The Lost Village of Stocks-in-Bowland

The locomotive named "Stocks"

People sometimes ask me what it was like to live in such an isolated place as Dalehead. I can only say that we were happy and contented with our lot. We knew our limitations and didn't strive for the unattainable.

Tom Cowking.

Where are now the merry party, I remember long ago—
Gathered round the kitchen fire, warmed by its ruddy glow?
They have all dispersed and wandered—far away, far away;
They have all dispersed and wandered—far away.

A Victorian song popular at Dalehead.

It must be hard to have your childhood haunts completely wiped from the face of the earth, under millions of gallons of water and acres of forest, as though they had never been. But the memories are still crystal clear...

Kaye Moon, in conversation with Vic Robinson.

The Lost Village
of
Stocks-in-Bowland

by W R Mitchell

(with line drawings by Peter Fox)

CASTLEBERG
1992

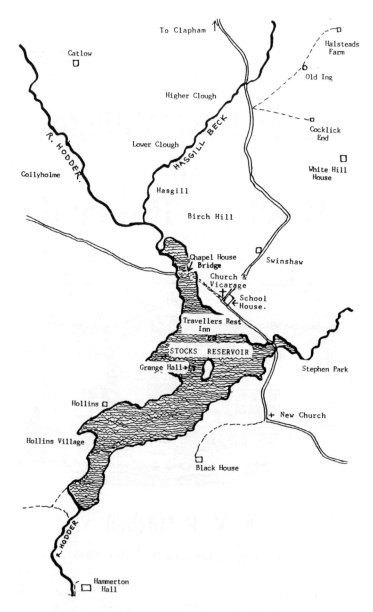

Published by Castleberg, 18 Yealand Avenue, Giggleswick,
Settle, North Yorkshire, BD24 0AY

Typeset in Clearface and printed by Lamberts Printers,
Station Road, Settle, North Yorkshire, BD24 9AA

ISBN: 1 871064 90 2

Contents

Acknowledgements

Clitheroe Advertiser, Clitheroe Reference Librarian, J Cooper, Tom and Alice Cowking, John Dewhurst, G Freeman, Bill Harrison, Geoff Harrison, George Horner, John Howden, Mrs M A Howard, J N King-Wilkinson, David MacNamee, Misses E and L Pickles, Eva Robinson, George Robinson, Vic and Annie Robinson, Kathleen Seed, Norman Swindlehurst, Percy Tilbury, Robert (Robin) and Ivy Waddington, Doris Wells, the Wilshaw family.

5

O Bolland, O Bolland,
Thy roads are rough
Thy people's manners worse:
To live in such a place
I would think it a curse.

*Found scratched on a window
at The Travellers' Rest, Stocks Fold.*

The area of the Hodder watershed is 9,259 acres and it has an average annual rainfall of 60 inches. The water is of excellent quality...

Fylde Water Board, 1932.

There isn't even a deserted village. Dalehead has gone and where the farmland of old is not drowned by the reservoir, it is covered with forest trees.

Frank Dugdale (1958).

Stocks in Bowland is not forgotten by many families. Stories of life there in the 1920s will continue to be told for generations to come.

Herbert Roberts (1975).

Today, Dalehead is sunk without trace, its church, vicarage, farm-houses and pub pulled down to make way for the three-mile long Stocks reservoir near Slaidburn...

A moorland church, built from the same stone as the original, together with the graves of 150 Dalehead people whose bodies were exhumed before the flooding, are all that is left of a tiny community chosen to make the ultimate sacrifice.

Graham Johnson, Lancashire Evening Post (1976).

Introduction

I BEGIN with the story of a parson and a sneck, which is an old-fashioned type of door latch.

The Rev T W Castle, who served in the parish of Stocks-in-Bowland, moved to wildest Canada, where he became an honorary chief of the Blackfoot Indians. He returned to live in retirement at the Yorkshire market town of Settle.

Mr Castle was "hard on himself". He believed that a truly fit person was one who covered ten miles a day on foot. When asked to help out in Austwick parish, where I was then living, he walked to and fro over Buckhaw Brow. He would never accept a lift in my car, even when the snow-dogs were howling.

One day, after he had tea with us in our old-fashioned cottage, he rose to leave for yet another stroll back to Settle. His fingers encountered our front door sneck. This reminded him of life at the Vicarage at Stocks-in-Bowland, an area which was flooded in the 1930s to create a reservoir for the Fylde district of Lancashire.

Mr Castle returned to his seat, accepted another cup of tea and told us of the days when salmon ran up to the headwaters of the Hodder to spawn in the gravel beds.

Poaching was rife when salmon were running. The fins of the lordly fish were visible as they wriggled through the shallows. Mr Cowking, who lived at Grange Hall, had a rough-haired collie called Tidy which grabbed passing salmon and brought them to the bank. Another farmer speared a 32 lb salmon—a stumpy fish with a wide tail—with the fork he was using for muck-spreading.

Everyone called to see that salmon, except the beck watcher, an elderly, bearded man who had been lured into the Hark to Bounty

7

at Slaidburn and rendered "market fresh".

In early autumn, the folk living near the upper Hodder went salmon-mad. They had all sorts of ways of cooking the fish. Sometimes the steaks were fried. Sometimes the salmon was boiled with parsley sauce. What could not be eaten was mashed up and served to the hens. The Daleheaders just couldn't cope.

They never stopped to think about the legality of their action. Mr Castle, new to the parish, stood up in the pulpit at Dalehead Church and denounced the widespread poaching.

On the following morning, as he prepared to leave the Vicarage, he found he could not lift the sneck of the back door. He had to leave by the front door. Hanging from the other side of the sneck, and weighing it down, was a prime salmon with a note: "Tak it and say nowt."

The old story came to mind recently in conversation with an Austwick friend. It seemed a pity to waste that tale or the many others I had heard over the years of life in what the romantics call "a drowned village".

They are referring to what is now known as Stocks-in-Bowland, a name bestowed on it by the Fylde Water Board who, early this century, acquired powers to compulsorily purchase 9,500 acres of the shallow basin of the upper Hodder, and did so at the bargain price of £150,000.

To the local people, this isolated district was simply "Dalehead", a much-loved area despite the heavy rainfall and claggy fellsides. A local tenant farmer, living on "next to nowt", was ignorant of the Water Board's intentions, for the negotiations were with the owners. When the first machines moved in, some people believed that they were preparing the ground for an Army camp.

The paperwork was being carried out before the 1914-18 war. In 1920, work began in earnest with the construction of a 13 mile long private railway (at a cost of £90,000) from Tosside to Greenfold Quarry and the site of the proposed dam. Twelve years later, the work was done. Scores of Daleheaders experienced an Exile which was every bit as heart-rending as that recorded in the Bible.

The Vicarage at Stocks, where Mr Castle found a sneckbound salmon, was just one of the casualties, being taken down, stone by stone, along with other buildings, and incorporated in The Board Room which cost £10,000 to build at its splendid site overlooking the new dam.

I stood on the Cross o' Greet Bridge and gazed at the infant Hodder, which was named by the Celtic folk, the name meaning "sparkling river". That day, it was tinged brown with peat. There was something Scottish in the sense of space, the brawling watercourse, the fells bonneted by cloud and the unfenced road, like a grey ribbon between fronds of bracken which had a coppery hue.

Soon the Hodder loses its identity and its spirit in Stocks Reservoir. Upstart conifers occupy most of the catchment area, where the bleating of sheep has been succeeded by the rasp of the chain saw. In the old days, meadows and pastures formed a green belt between dun-coloured moors. Alders stood at the edge of the river. Magnificent lime trees were to be seen near the stepping stones.

The farms of Dalehead were squandered [well distributed] across an undulating landscape. Field divisions were of drystone walls or thorn-hedges. What is now an island, the nesting place of black-headed gulls, was a hillock near the late lamented Grange Hall—a hillock containing a mush of clay and boulders, a legacy of the last Ice Age.

Many visitors to Stocks arrive when there is a drought. They are lured here by tales that the "lost" village of Stocks has reappeared. An imaginative story is told of the clanging of the church bell.

What the visitor sees are acres of mud which have been colonised by plants, giving an illusion of farmland. Chapel House bridge re-appears along with pieces of stone, all that were left by the crawler tractors and draglines as the reservoir was being shaped.

Dalehead Church was demolished and re-built, minus the chancel, on a site well above high water mark. Nearly everything else connected with Stocks was re-cycled and is no longer recognisable.

Grass, trees and brambles obscure the embankments and cuttings of the narrow gauge railways on which were shifted supplies and the stone needed to line the dam. Ramblers walking west of the Hodder use a section of the trackbed which was laid for the line used for conveying stone from Jumbles Quarry, where the equipment included a steam crane.

Old Mr Castle, who served the parish of Dalehead, may have appreciated some of the wilderness quality of what is now Stocks Reservoir. With its fringe of conifers, it is not unlike a Canadian lake, especially when several hundred Canada geese are stirring. Having rested or preened by the water, they fly with resonant honking calls to graze on the best fields.

Wigeon, bird refugees from northern lands, enliven the winter days with cheery whistles. Autumn is the time of the sika deer rut, when stags in forest glades announce their presence to the hinds by uttering several high-pitched squeals. From a distance, these are like the whistling of a northern Pan. The hoarse bark of a roebuck may also be heard where, within living memory, the ground was occupied by Shorthorn cattle and horned sheep.

It is over 30 years since I first became aware of the extraordinary birdlife of Stocks Reservoir. The estate foreman of the time was P J Kean, who photographed the first nesting pair of Canada geese. They had selected a corner of the island. By the time I led a small party of the Austwick Field Club to Stocks, and Mr Kean took us by boat to the island, the place was a mass of squawking gulls. We moved in a blizzard of white wings.

When I decided to collect stories of old Dalehead, I found myself following a tradition set by Frank Dugdale, the Clitheroe journalist who returned again and again to the theme of Stocks-in-Bowland in articles published weekly in the *Lancashire Evening Post*.

At Slaidburn show, in 1957, he chatted with H Cottam, who had been the resident engineer from the beginning of the reservoir scheme. (During the 1939-45 war, Mr Cottam was officer commanding the local Home Guard, which spent part of its time looking for the wrecks of aircraft which had crashed on the Bowland fells).

Twenty years later, Graham Johnson, writing in the same newspaper, in somewhat more racy style, was reporting on a chat he had with John Heap, the cost clerk and cashier for the Fylde Water Board who later became the Board's chief administrative officer.

"By the time Prince George opened the reservoir in 1932, John Heap had seen more than 30 farms demolished...and handed over thousands of wage packets to the hard-drinking gangers and tried to sort out hundreds of domestic troubles...

"Navvies imported from all over Britain for the big dig were rationed to two pints of beer each lunch-time. Hard liquor was banned altogether, but they made up for it by drinking enough beer and stout to sink a battleship...

"Some of them cooked plenty of kippers to give themselves a thirst. Drink accounted for a fair chunk of their £2.5s a week wage, but out of that they had to pay for food and board."

The very mention of Dalehead to the octogenarians I met released a flood of memories, from schooldays when (in wet weather) so many clothes were draped from the guard around the stove "you couldn't see anything for steam rising," to the long trudge to a local dance, latterly in wellingtons, which were doffed and left, upside down, in a handy spot, the dancers proceeding in their best footwear.

Tom Cowking had been among those who enjoyed a slide show organised by emissaries of the Church Army who arrived in a horse-drawn caravan adorned by short Biblical quotations. The slide show took place in the School, the projector being connected to a supply of acetylene gas.

At the shanty village of Hollins, during "reservoir time", the cinema had proved an irresistible, twice-a-week attraction for young people from the farms, who watched with drooping lower jaws such epics as *Rin Tin Tin.*

Vic Robinson, another Daleheader with an almost photographic memory of t'owd times, mentioned when raising sheep was "a lot of hard work for nothing." At Stephen Park, the lambs were born in April and by autumn the spare lambs were being driven to Copy Nook, near Bolton-by-Bowland, for sale. "There was no motor transport then—and if there had been we couldn't have afforded it."

The best offer for the lambs might be 11s each, which was unacceptable to father, so the lambs were driven back to Stephen Park. Another day, they were driven to a "place near the old tithe barn at Slaidburn, where they might get 15s. We'd sell 'em at that."

Vic recalled the Dalehead "clippings", when young lads caught the sheep and dragged them towards the clippers. "At Catlow, Ted Robinson used to come and keep 'em in order. He also used to catch. I've seen Ted go down that shippon and bring two sheep back, one under each arm for t'clippers.

"He'd say: 'Who wants one?' A clipper would shout: 'Bring it here: I'm nearly clipped off.' Bill Tillotson used to go round marking sheep when they let 'em off t'stock. We used to look forrard to clipping-time."

As soon as the men arrived at Catlow, they went into the house, donned their overalls and had something to eat—mostly sandwiches and cakes, which were easy to carry out into the barn.

"We used to arrange it so that we could stop there all day and clip away. There'd be joke-telling and we pulled each other's leg. When we finished, at seven o'clock, sometimes later, and we had let the sheep go, then we'd all go and have a wash. Dishes of water were arranged on a wall-top for the men to use. Then there'd be more to eat. And I can tell you, we didn't want any more that day!"

In the 1930s, four Dalehead men who were nifty clippers travelled to Bradford and snipped the jackets from a group of sheep to start off the process of making a suit within 24 hours. The adroit clippers, Ted and Jack Robinson, Hector Beck and Jack Greenwood, brought some suits home with them!

The clippers and their families kept unsociable hours. Eva Robinson relates that at Catlow, the day ended with a dance in the barn. The floor was not particularly smooth but as the men wore big boots it did not matter so much. Non-dancers sat on bales of hay. The dance continued until daybreak.

Doris Wells of Rimington needed no encouragement to return to her native Dalehead—to the farm where she was born and to the site of Church, School and Vicarage. She pointed to a gate enmeshed in barbed wire and bits of old railtrack and observed that this was on the old road to the village. In her young days, money was scarce—but scarcely needed in a community where frugal living and mutual helpfulness were general.

We visited the "new" Church, which at that time was dressed overall for the Harvest Festival (though the bell no longer summons the worshippers, having been stolen). She recalled when farm men gathered at the Church. "I will not say they always attended a service, but they were always there when we came out!"

Doris was reared at Halsteads, which was a tidy distance to walk to attend School and Church. On Sunday, she and her young friends followed a field path to the roadside and, leaving their clogs behind a wall, donned shoes for the last stretch, which was downhill on the road.

Over 60 years before her return to Dalehead, Doris and her brother had varied the journey by walking along the tops of the walls, passing the site of an older school which their father had attended.

Doris recalled the excitement caused when the first motor vehicles appeared. A motor car drew up outside *The Travellers' Rest* at Stocks Fold in 1919. Excitement arose from the departure of a vicar who had hired a large motor vehicle to move his possessions, for "when they started the engine, it struck fire. They soon put the fire out."

A Dalehead childhood had its heartaches and also its blissful moments—such as when Doris and her brother sat on the granary steps, cracking the shells of newly-gathered hazel nuts with a stone. Mother had encouraged them to go nutting. She gave them strong blue bags—the sort the grocer used for weighing out sugar and raisins—for the nuts. Cracking open the shells could be painful if the stone was not aimed correctly.

Dalehead had a bountiful wild life, including trout in the river and rabbits on every bit of under-farmed land. One wet haytime, when no outdoor work could be done for many days, Doris's dad went off fishing and Sam, the haytime man [from County Durham] "catched rabbits."

For a week or two, the family lived on fish and rabbits. "Young rabbits were good. Mother cooked them with a bacon joint. The rabbit improved the taste of the bacon. We nearly lived off bacon! And the bacon improved the rabbit."

Dalehead has its own weather pattern, with the accent on rain. Doris relates: "One day we got absolutely soaked through. When we came home, the folk at the next farm had a load of hay. Not a drop of rain had fallen there. We'd been rained off—and had got wet into the bargain."

It was Doris who told me the moving story of a time over 70 years before, when Mr and Mrs Taylor and their four children lived at Old Ing. They had only one meadow and a large pasture. One morning, as Doris went to school through the fields, she saw a group of people outside Old Ing. Mrs Taylor was wearing a coat over her nightgown.

That evening, Doris asked her mother about the mysterious little group of people and was told that "a horse couldn't have its foal and it's died." Subsequently, Doris's father handed over sixpence and asked her to get a notebook from the village shop. If any money remained, she might get some sweets but "share 'em among t'other kids."

Over the years, Doris often thought about the notebook and why dad had wanted it. "It was not till after mother died in 1977 that I came across that notebook again. After the Taylors lost their one and only horse, dad went round the farmers for donations so that he could buy them a new horse. Doris concluded her tale by saying, vehemently: "Would they do it today? That was the way we lived..."

Vic Robinson grew up on a farm where high priority was given to horses. "My father had horsitis. We always had about ten or a dozen young horses about us. We used to break 'em in and then sell 'em. You'd make £30 or £40 on a horse." That was a bit of help to us."

A horse being "broken in" had breaking-gears fitted for about a fortnight. "There was a big thick bit with flanges inside so that the horse kept chewing them. When a horse had a proper mouth, you could do anything with it."

Re-telling stories of life at Dalehead made many an old 'un feel young again. Tale after tale tumbled from the lockers of their minds. Those were the days of big families, including one at Tosside where sixteen children were born. "There were four sets o' twins, you know. So that's half of 'em... Some twins in our family died, otherwise we'd have had sixteen, too."

Eva Robinson (nee Walmsley) was one of a family of nine children, seven of whom she "brought up" at Black House following the death of her mother. Eva, like many another pupil at Dalehead, left school at the age of thirteen. "We had always had a servant girl before that. We never had one when I stopped going to school."

I heard of the days when her father went to Lancaster to hire a new girl to work in the house. A shilling was handed over to "fasten" her. "The last one he hired never turned up. He wrote a sharp letter and said he was going to put her in court. She sent the shilling back..."

The same Irishman came year after year to help with haytime. Mother gave him oddments of clothing she no longer needed for her children, though she herself had little of this world's goods, and the Irishman promised that he would let her have a goose.

It arrived not long after he had been to Black House for what turned out to be the last time. The goose was delivered unpacked; there was just some string and a label round its neck!

In my quest for information, I was privileged to look into faded photograph albums of Dalehead families. "That was my dad," said an old lady. "He was in the Army. First world war. He was a big tall chap. He came back to us but he'd got malaria. He had attacks for years, you know. The bed used to shake when he had an attack."

The next photograph was of Dalehead (old) church. "It was a shame they had to pull it down. It was a nice little church..." Another print showed dalesfolk on an outing to Blackpool. It was from Wigglesworth, not Dalehead, and (photographically) "it shouldn't be among 'em." Nor should one of a day trip by charabanc from Tosside. "It took you nearly all day to get theer..."

We resurrected ancient tittle-tattle. Mr Starkie, the gamekeeper, lived at Kenibus. When Mrs Parker of Collyholme went to Catlow to help nurse John Robinson, who had diphtheria, she died of that grim disease.

Tom Cowking, the source of many wonderful tales, mentioned his Uncle William, of Lamb Hill, and his dog Blackie, which was persuaded to catch the old cockerel, just for a joke. Tom also told me of the terrible spring of 1917, when snow lay all spring and decked the top of Pendle Hill in summer. With the sheep short of milk, lambing time was difficult. The calves developed "husk" from eating poor quality hay. "But we survived."

He also told me of the insensitivity of officials of the Fylde Water Board. As I have related, the local people were not fully informed of what was about to happen to their homes and the land they had farmed. Because they were tenants, there was no mention of compensation.

Tom's widowed mother and their five children were in a horse-drawn car, en route for their new home, and feeling a sense of deprivation, when two officials of the Board who were staying in the comparative luxury of *The Travellers' Rest* hotel noticed some old straw in the bottom of the cart. It was very old straw, suitable for "bedding down" stock.

In due course, an official letter arrived from head office at Blackpool demanding an explanation and stating what the penality was for such a crime!

Mother had the last word. The arrival of the letter coincided with Dalehead Sports, which the two Water Board officials had decided to visit. Mother approached them in front of a crowd and gave them a piece of her mind.

They had no option but to apologise.

In The Beginning

THE story of the Hodder Valley began some 360 million years ago, when most of the land mass known as Britain lay much further south than it is today. The limestone which is now the core of the area was formed in a clear sea bright with corals and sea-lilies (crinoids). The remains of these creatures slowly accumulated on the bed of the sea and were compressed into the familar grey rock.

Muddy water, caused by material from a land mass to the north, led to the formation of a "blue" type of limestone. In due course, the deltaic conditions and luxuriant plant growth were responsible for the Bowland Shales. Finally, around 130 million years ago, the deposition of sand led to the formation of gritstones.

In geologically recent times, the Ice Age developed. Ice, advancing from Lakeland into Craven split up like fingers from a hand. One finger entered what is now the Hodder valley and gouged it out, coating the lower slopes with a mush we call boulder-clay.

The ice melted about 15,000 years ago, leaving a glacial lake. Ice dams broke. The heady rush of melt-water down the Hodder created the gorge near Whitewell. Weathering of the millstone grit at Bowland Knotts and Whelpstone Crag produced smooth shapes, like gigantic molars.

Celtic folk named many of our northern rivers, including the Hodder, Wyre and Lune. They may have named the district of Craven, within which Dalehead lies.

The Angles, immigrants from the Continent, spread west and, by the middle of the seventh century were well established in the lower country. These people—the first English—may have named

A Bridge at Dalehead.

the River Ribble after ripel (a boundary).

An energetic people, the Angles founded "ton" settlements, as at Newton and Waddington; they cleared away areas of native forest in the lower Hodder and Ribble valleys. Their heavy ploughs ripped the strong soils.

At Dalehead, the land was cold and wet, better suited to pastoral farming. So it was that, a thousand years ago, a few Irish-Norse families arrived from the west and established small farms. The map of Bowland was subsequently peppered with Norse terms, such as fell, dale, beck, crag, gill and moss.

The name Tosside is said to be derived from tod (a fox) and "side" from saeter, the summer pasture ground of Norse folk who took their cattle and other domestic animals upbank in the warmer months to make use of the flush of grass and to allow the meadowland at home to grow grass for conversion into hay, the winter fodder for the stock.

Before the Conquest, Dalehead was in the vast parish of Whalley. When the Normans took over, and the new landowner was Robert de Lacy, churches were founded. A church at Slaidburn reduced in size the parish of Whalley and brought the Daleheaders closer to a place of worship.

The Normans heaped gifts of land on to the monasteries. Among the outlying granges [farms] associated with Kirkstall was Rushton in Bowland, almost forty miles from the Abbey.

Kirkstall came into the possession of Rushton from Robert de Lacy in 1180. He also provided the monks with pasture for 160 mares and their two-yearlings and for 200 cows with their three-year-old offspring. Further grants of land from this family (1220 and 1235) converted Rushton into a considerable estate covering the upper Hodder valley to the watershed with the Wenning.

In the fourteenth century, the bounds of the Forest of Bowland contracted, the jurisdiction of Forest officials previously extending to the Hodder basin. The Forest was not a forest in the modern sense, of massed trees. The word foras relates to land set apart for hunting. Bowland became a Royal forest in which a king never hunted.

The Hammertons of Hammerton Hall, which stands close to the Hodder, were the medieval big-wigs. By judicious marriages, the Hammertons acquired so much land they were said to be able to ride to York without leaving the family property.

In the Church at Slaidburn, virtually the family history of the Wilkinsons is written on memorial tablets, one of which relates that members of this family moved to Slaidburn and Dalehead from Hellifield in 1626. Their previous home was Hellifield Peel.

They settled at Swinshaw and, having a goodly number of sons who found pleasure in acquiring land and property, they became considerable landowners.

The Anglican outpost was Houghton Chapel, at Tosside, and in the mid-17th century, it was recommended that the chapel should become a parish church "and have some maintenance annexed, being entirely dependent on the benevolence of the people." (Nothing happened until 1870 when the old chapel was given its parish status and dedicated to St Bartholomew).

Towards the end of the eighteenth and in the early part of the nineteenth centuries, the great enclosure movement took place. Land on which there had been common rights was parcelled up, divided by fences and drystone walls. The walls, made of random stone, gave the landscape a tidier appearance and enabled local people to improve their methods of farming.

For official purposes, Dalehead was divided into three unequal parts—Easington, Gisburn Forest and the Higher Division of Bowland Forest.

Dalehead began to show its increasing importance in the nineteenth century. It was basically a farming community, with a few large farms and many farms where the tenants did little more than subsist. Large families were the rule.

Grange Hall Farm, in the Hodder basin, was a reminder through its name of the old-time benevolence of the de Lacys to the monks of Kirkstall Abbey. The Cowkings of Grange Hall are thought to be descendants of Huguenots (immigrant French Protestants).

On an Ordnance map of 1843 Grange Hall is shown to have a corn mill which was driven by water power from the Hodder. In due course, one of the millstones was erected as part of a monument outside the entrance gates of the hall.

The early nineteenth century saw the rise of Nonconformity, fuelled by Anglican priests who, because they refused to conform to everything in the Book of Common Prayer, were ejected from their livings. Some of these displaced parsons were made welcome in Bowland.

The Rev Benjamin Sowden, who became minister at Horton-in-

Craven, held house services in various places, including Higher Sandy Syke, the home of Miles Thornber, where in course of time over 200 people gathered for worship.

A place of worship was built. Mount Zion chapel, opened in 1813, has been scarcely altered. Benjamin Sowden, who entertained hopes of becoming the minister, was so disappointed at the appointment of another that he fell ill and died.

An Ordnance map of 1843 shows the original Dalehead school stood just above Swinshaw Farm, beside the road to Bowland Knotts.

Not for many years had Swinshaw been able to accommodate all the Wilkinsons. The family was now well represented at Slaidburn and at the beginning of the century, William and Leonard had town houses in Blackburn. They founded a well-known firm of solicitors which bore their names.

The Anglican cause was rejuvenated at Dalehead in mid-century (1852) when a church was built and dedicated to St James. The site of church and parsonage was given by William Wilkinson, of Hellifield, who also endowed it with the sum of £50 annually, derived from his farm at Kettlesbeck. This William [one of many Williams, for it was a popular family name] died on June 10, 1860.

In 1871, Dalehead became a separate ecclesiastical parish, hewn from part of the huge parish of Slaidburn, and in July, 1875, the Wilkinson family presented the Church with a large font. The Kings and the Wilkinsons were united in marriage. The former family had owned land mainly at Aysgarth and also for a time they held the title deeds to Whiteholme at Slaidburn (a house built by King-Birchall).

The King-Wilkinson crest features unicorns and the motto, "Ne Quid Nimis", which may be translated "not too much of anything" (literally, in today's idiom, "a little of what you fancy does you good"!).

At about this time, most of the 300 people at Dalehead lived at widely scattered farms. Although it was tucked out of sight of the world, Dalehead was not a cul de sac. Roads converging on the main village [a few assorted buildings] bifurcated, one branch going via the Cross o' Greet and the Great Stone of Fourstone to High Bentham and the other route linking Bolton-by-Bowland with Clapham by way of Bowland Knotts.

The roads were "waterbound", the constituents being mud and stones which were broken up by the local roadman or someone who had contracted to do the job as "piece work". Roadman were paid by results.

Over Bowland Knotts went local people with horses and carts, intent on collecting coal from the colliery at Ingleton. The doctor at Clapham was the handiest in case of emergency—and if the weather was kind.

Each road had its scattering of tradesmen and salesmen, emissaries of grocers, also butter badgers and itinerant tailors who, staying at a farmhouse for a day or two, sat in their customary cross-legged pose, making up clothes for the farm folk, who provided food and accommodation.

Hospitality was available at *The New Inn,* which in 1892 was owned by Thomas Robinson. It was extended at the start of the new century and by 1903 came into the possession of John Swale. The inn's licence had been relinquished and the place was named *The Travellers' Rest.*

It continued to be a gathering place for travellers and had a good reputation for catering for wedding meals. Those in the know might drink something stronger than lemonade. The innkeeper's son, Tom, married Isabella Parker from Bolton-by-Bowland.

The acid land around Dalehead was sweetened by applications of limestone imported from lower down the Hodder Valley, where the rock outcropped and was burnt using field kilns. Tom Cowking, born at Dalehead in 1904, recalls when two limekilns were operating in the district—one at Raingill Farm and the other at Hammerton Hall.

Broken into suitable sizes, the stone was transported to the kiln, to be packed with alternating layers of coal (which then was sixpence a hundredweight). When the kiln died down, the limestone was raked out and carted away to make "lime and earth", several tons being mixed together and left until it fell to powder. The heap was turned several times to blend the material and then it was carted on to the land. "No other fertiliser was known in those days."

Leonard King-Wilkinson, of Middlewood, startled his neighbours when he first toured the area in a De Dion steam car. Years later, he described it to Tom Cowking: "It was fired by paraffin burners. If I gave it time to blow off steam at the bottom of a hill it would usually have the power to get to the top."

At the turn of the century, Jules Hirst, a wealthy cotton manufacturer with a house in Scotland had the shooting rights over most of Dalehead and the family rented Town Head at Slaidburn (until the late 1930s).

Jules was succeeded by his son, Colonel Hirst, who was chairman of Coats' Cotton in Glasgow (and also had a mill in Skipton). The Hirsts had a resident housekeeper who "lived in". The family also owned Lamb Hill.

The King-Wilkinson family gave £100 to buy the silver-plated instruments for the Slaidburn Band, which periodically visited Dalehead.

In 1912, the Fylde Water Board obtained Parliamentary powers to construct waterworks and reservoirs in the upper Hodder Valley. Work was somewhat delayed by the 1914-18 war, a time when most of the young men were in the Forces.

A proportion of each farm was ploughed up by young men temporarily released from the Forces because of their specialist skills. Tom Cowking, then at New House Farm, watched the arrival of a man with two horses and a wagon containing hay and cereals [for the animals] and a plough.

This young soldier rose at 5 a.m. to attend to the horses and he then set about ploughing, the land being devoted to corn which grew well but did not ripen satisfactorily and was eventually fed to the stock.

As usual, war hastened technological developments. A Canadian "Sunshine" tractor appeared at Lamb Hill. The local joiner, who had an oil engine to drive a circular saw, adapted the engine to grind corn.

The most profound changes took place during the main reservoir-building period (1923 to 1932).This period also saw the shrinking of the large King-Wilkinson estate, which until 1927 consisted of about 50 farms in the Hodder Valley. Subsequently, the family had only one farm at Dalehead, this being Raingill, which the family bought back from All Soul's College after the 1939-45 war.

The reason why the family's fortunes waned was the second of the "cotton slumps", when William King-Wilkinson, of Slaidburn, lost a great deal of money in cotton futures.

The construction of the dam for the reservoir which the Fylde Water Board called Stocks led to the flooding of 244 acres of pasture and made it necessary for the hamlet and several farms to be demolished. Additionally, twenty-six farms and cottages on the catchment area had to be abandoned.

The Hodder's riparian owners were provided with compensation water, but since the reservoir was opened the quantity of water released has been halved, then halved again. It was originally 28 million gallons of water a day. During the 1950s, it declined to 14 million gallons and and now the flow is seven million gallons a day. No fish pass was built, so any migrant fish [salmon and sea trout] have to spawn on the river bed below the dam.

For a time, the Robinson family rented 1,500 acres of land extending from Stephen Park to Brown Hills and ran sheep here. Then, in 1948, the Forestry Commission took over. Afforestation with conifers was rapidly introduced. The upper valley of the Hodder, once a pastoral area, now has affinities with the Canadian Backwoods.

The Travellers' Rest.

Village Life

An old photograph shows Stocks Fold looking rather dead. I wish there had been a picture of the Fold showing all the horses and traps there when Harry Taylor came over from Holden to buy butter and eggs.

Frank Dugdale (1957).

The Travellers' Rest was a temperance hotel but you could always get a jar there. It wasn't broadcast.

A Daleheader in Exile (1992).

IN THE days before the Fylde Water Board put in a claim for the heavy rainfall of the upper Hodder valley, the unmetalled road from Slaidburn to Stocks-in-Bowland took a leisurely course between grey walls formed of random stones.

At Grange Farm, a highway which was dusty in dry weather and puddly when it rained, made a smart turn to the left and passed Low Barn. This is remembered as having a substantial porch, in the Craven style, the porch being large enough to accommodate a load of hay still on the cart if the weather suddenly worsened and it had to be rushed under cover.

Low Barn stood with its back to the Hodder, the banks of which were decked with trees, including four limes of magnificent girth. The hillock beyond the river was a drumlin, left by a long-melted glacier. One might cross the Hodder using stepping stones.

When salmon were running, a tremor of excitement could be felt throughout the valley. The poacher took his share of the bounty of salmon, operating mainly at night, enticing the fish towards the gaff by shining a light on the water. The poacher's technique was first to lure the bailiff away so "tha knew where tha'd got him."

The salmon poacher tried to become as inconspicuous as a shadow. He moved in the gloaming, when the fluty call of the otter was heard above the ripple of the Hodder. There was always a chance of being "nabbed", which added to the excitement. "I got a bit o' satisfaction out of doing summat I'd every right to do—but which t'law of t'land said I mustn't do." This man collected 70 "nice fish" on a poaching expedition.

Grange Hall and its attendant little wood occupied an area where the Pleistocene ice-sheet had left a gravel bed. The land was free-draining and did not poach (become puddly).

Stocks-in-Bowland

The eye of the traveller ranged beyond Grange Hall to the village, if such it could be described, which lay 11 miles from the market town of Clitheroe. Here was the inn, post office, stores and smithy. The place had only two dwellings, one above the shop and the other at the inn. A little to the north were the Church, Vicarage and the School, with an adjacent house for the head-master.

Stocks-in-Bowland or Stocks Fold, tucked out of sight of the world, was accessible from Tossit (Tosside), Bolton-by-Bowland or Slaidburn. A greater effort was needed to visit the place using one of the moorland routes from Bentham or Clapham, in the Wenning Valley.

The travellers of many years ago were as varied and interesting as Chaucer's pilgrims to Canterbury. Hawkers were numerous. Gipsies sold pegs or inquired at the farms for fallen wool, rabbit or mole skins. An odd-job man sought temporary work, such as scaling muck in the pastures.

Tramps begged food and drink before kipping (sleeping) in a barn. Tom Cowking got the shock of his life when, calling at a out-barn to "fother" the cows, while on his way to school, he reached for an armful of hay from the heap which his father had left for him on the previous day. Curled up in the hay was a tramp. "He didn't say a word and neither did I."

Paying guests at *The Travellers' Rest* included representatives of two Bentham clothing firms—Fishers and Garlicks. When the Walmsleys left the village shop for Black House Farm, mother developed scarlet fever and was promptly taken to the isolation hospital at Harden Bridge, Austwick, where the first person she saw was the son of the Garlicks—a lad who had recently stayed at Black House.

Road Traffic

The sounds of the horse-drawn vehicles were distinctive. The axles of some traps slammed against the wheel bushes. This form of transport was used by farmers and their wives going to market. Tom Cowking's grandmother, concerned at the rough surface of the road, insisted that the children sat in the trap bottom in case they were tossed out.

Over the moorland roads came horses with carts laden with coal, a luxury which was used sparingly, the main fuel being peat cut on the moors. "Peat warmed thee twice—once when you were cutting it and once when it kept the home fire burning on a winter's neet."

Most of the rural folk walked. They developed a steady, untiring pace which ate up the miles. Men, women and the bairns were accustomed to walking and, because life then was nowhere near as hectic as it is today, they were content to take their time over a journey.

Medical Services

The nearest doctor, who lived at Clapham, beyond Bowland Knotts, was rarely summoned for illnesses because he charged for his services. "He was called out when a bairn was due to be born, though an old lady stood by to help and sometimes she was the midwife as well. I still marvel how they managed to get an urgent message to the doctor."

One doctor, who rarely hurried, was said to arrive for a birth when the child was ready to start school! Home remedies were used. In spring, children were given weekly doses of sulphur and treacle.

Tom Forrest, the dentist, toured the area pulling teeth. Doris Wells (nee Carr) recalls that "he did my mother's teeth." A pair of do-it-yourself tooth-pullers could be borrowed from Owlshaw, near Whelpstone Crag.

The doctor who, three years before, had delivered Doris at White Hill House, presumed that the Carrs were still at the farm when he was called out again. "My grandparents had moved down to White Hill House and Heber, an unmarried son, was living at home.

"Though it was June, by the time the doctor rode his horse to White Hill House it was dark. In those days, the doors of farms were never locked. Yon doctor walked into the house and straight upstairs, He entered the first bedroom he came to, and it was Uncle Heber's, who had to get dressed and take the doctor up to Thorsteard [Halsteads]."

Visiting Tradesmen

On Thursday, which was market day at Stocks Fold, Harry Taylor travelled up from Holden with provender and groceries. He also sold oatcakes and muffins. Much bartering took place. The farm folk traded their produce—eggs, butter, cheese and rabbits—for necessities.

Long before the "milk cheque" became a cornerstone of a farmer's economy, he hand-milked his cows and separated the cream from the milk by pouring it into a lead [a shallow metal tray]. In due course, the "blue" milk could be drained away and the cream clung to the sides of the lead and was scraped into a crock till churning day, when it was converted into butter.

The quality varied according to the herbage grazed by the cows. If a round pound of butter was made, each producer had a distinctive wooden stamp (made of sycamore, which did not taint the butter).

Tom Cowking recalls Aunt Betty taking over the process as the butter appeared in the churn. She worked and moulded it until all the buttermilk had been extracted, then patted it into 1 lb blocks with the "Scotch Hands" and stored it until a cart belonging to Dugdales of Holden collected it.

The Hanson family of Raingill Farm went into butter-making in a big way and each week in June, when the grass was at its best and milk production peaked, they had a hundredweight of butter awaiting collection.

Tom remembers when one of the men from Grange Hall visited New Close once a week to collect cream—two buckets full of cream—which was churned along with that produced at the Grange.

The butter made at Dalehead was retailed in the Colne and Nelson districts. The dealers who lived at Holden had grim tales to tell of journeys on the road from Gisburn to Nelson at snowtime.

Imports at Dalehead included barrels of beer from Dennis Byrne, the Clitheroe grocer, some of the barrels ordered in summer being for the benefit of haytime workers. Byrnes also distributed groceries, orders being taken by their traveller, Harry Simpson.

Vic Robinson, who was brought up at Stephen Park, says that orders placed with Byrnes were delivered by Tommy Bleasdale, using a flat cart with two horses, one of which had a rat tail (it lacked hairs).

Of the firms operating out of Settle, two were well-known at Dalehead, these being Tathams the grocers and Shepherd and Walker, who supplied veterinary requirements and medicines.

Travelling drapers included Abraham Roberts, Alfred Ingham and Johnny Tomlinson (from Clitheroe), Garlicks (Bentham) and Gorrills and Lyon (of Lancaster).

Among the items brought on Dugdales cart was yeast, used in the making of bread. Tom Cowking says that if the bread ran out, and no yeast was available, mother made flapjacks in the frying pan. "We children welcomed the change, especially if currants were added to the mixture."

Mr Popay, the greengrocer at Long Preston, had a Slaidburn round. If an arrangement was made by a Dalehead family to meet him at the Crossroads, he took away any surplus pig meat, paying eightpence a pound. Or he might exchange meat for fish, cockles and mussels.

Pork Products

Everyone kept a pig or two and most people called on Stephen Robinson when there was a porker to be slaughtered. He killed the pig one day and returned in due course to cut it up. Pigs were well-fed, "not swill-fed, same as they are today." They received generous amounts of oatmeal.

"At our place," recalls Vic Robinson, "we always got a couple of bags of flour, which was JGB (John Greenwood, Blackburn). If it didn't just suit my mother, she'd say: 'Tak that to t'pigs. It's gone a bit fusty'." Pigs received plenty of milk. "That was a real bacon pig; it tasted of bacon when you killed it."

Usually, a pig about to be killed was laid on a pig-stock (a sort of bench). "We had a sor box (for liquid manure) which had never been used for years. It was not so big. We lifted the pig on to it and tied its legs." From the pig came meat which was hung in the kitchen, customarily from seven large hooks, accounting for two flitches, two hams, two shoulders and some pig-cheek. "Pig head was very nice if it was done right."

Vic says: "We always got our beef from Pearson Lumley, of Long Preston. It was off Aberdeen Angus cattle. He had these black pollies in a field. He gave them cake. When they were slaughtered, that *was* meat!"

The Travellers' Rest

John Swale, the joiner and wheelwright at Dalehead, worked behind the *New Inn,* then run by T C Robinson. Irishmen, in the dale to help with haytime, were fond of gathering there, sitting in groups and filling their tin mugs from a nine-gallon barrel of beer [cost, eight shillings] until it had been drained.

John Swale became the tenant of the inn. Mine host was often heard lamenting that he could not make a living from the inn alone, even allowing for the fact that some land went with it and so he might do a little farming as well.

The brewers, Messrs Crabtree of Clitheroe, decided to buy some additional acres which came on the market. What happened then provides an entertaining story, which was told by Frank Dugdale over 30 years ago.

"As it happened, John Swale had his eye on this extra land, too, and when the sale was held at *The Swan* at Clitheroe, everybody who was there knew that the only bidders would be Messrs Crabtree and Swale. These two got talking before the auction, Mr Crabtree wanting to know the strength of the competition.

"Mr Swale would not say what he might bid and when Mr Crabtree enlarged on the difficulties of the innkeeper and the lack of profit of the brewers, Mr Swale had the temerity to suggest that if things were as bad as all that, Mr Crabtree would be well advised to get rid of the inn.

"He said he only wished he could. The upshot was that John Swale bought it there and then. He got the extra land cheaply—and went home to tell the tale."

The new owner, not wishing to have anything to do with intoxicants, surrendered the licence and re-named the inn. He moved the Post Office from his little shop across the way.

The Travellers' Rest, strategically placed at the meeting of three roads, became well-known to the business traveller, who might get a bed for the night, a stable for his horse and some good meals.

Here, as photographs in old albums show, wedding receptions were held. The inn provided an interesting backdrop for the groups of relatives and friends. And here were the doleful gatherings after funerals held at Dalehead Church. Funeral cards were distributed, along with special biscuits and cups of hot tea to offset the chill picked up in a draughty churchyard.

Before the 1914-18 war, the inn became a home from home for Fylde Water Boards officials on preparatory jaunts connected with the reservoir. To the Daleheaders, these emissaries from head office at Blackpool seemed very sophisticated and they undoubtedly impressed the local people by the size and quality of their motor cars.

Over the Counter

John and Lily Walmsley, who kept the village shop, were known far and wide. John Walmsley was the Dalehead Poo-bah, forever busy in a variety of ways. John was a cobbler who was especially active during the first world war. He was also an adroit operator with brush, soap and razor, being the local barber.

His church offices included those of warden and, for nine years, of organist. He served as a School manager, was the parish clerk, and supported the Reading Room. His love of music extended to membership of Slaidburn brass band and he played the fiddle at dances. He dabbled in farming, having a few acres between the village and the school.

It is recalled that at the shop "you could buy sweets, tobacco and newspapers, bacon [cut by hand] and paraffin." John, who had a large family, was occasionally heard to remark that his children "ate all the profit!" Mrs Walmsley baked bread for the Vicar and the Schoolmaster. At the shop, you might collect copies of *Clitheroe Advertiser* or *Craven Herald*.

If the schoolchildren had any money, they would call at the stores at the mid-day break and buy "pop" in a type of bottle which had a marble as a stopper. If a half empty bottle was shaken vigorously and suddenly upended, the gas caused the stopper to fly back into place. The remaining pop was kept in a lively condition for later consumption.

If the impression is given of total rural tranquillity at Stocks, then it should be noted that on three occasions the shop premises were "broken into" and goods were stolen. Eighty years ago, when the Walmsleys had a small (and noisy) child, a break-in took place on a night when, for a change, the baby was on good behaviour and the whole family slept soundly.

The thieves, requiring early warning of anyone who might decide to descend the staircase from the bedrooms, collected the weights from the scales and placed them in buckets, which were then left on the stairs for someone to stumble over. They ransacked the shop. Post Office documents were dumped in the ash-pit outside.

Eva Robinson, the daughter of John Walmsley's daughter and granddaughter of Jane Swale, wife of the proprietor of *The Travellers' Rest*, has clear memories of the little shop. The Walmsleys moved to Black House. When Eva's mother died, nine children survived her. Two sons were married. Eva, being the eldest at home, devoted herself to bringing up the remainder. Happily, it was a large farmhouse, with five bedrooms.

Eva's mother told her tales of Stocks Ball, which was held annually in an outbuilding, with music provided by two violinists and a pianist. A dancer from Tosside wore evening dress and white gloves. It was said that the Carrs of White Hill House could, by themselves, make up a set for The Lancers.

At the Smithy

Mr Cornthwaite, the resident blacksmith, shod the horses of the upper dale, making and fitting the wrought iron shoes and blinking as he held a hot piece of metal against a hoof and was enveloped by acrid fumes. The longest queues were to be seen before haytime.

The blacksmith also hooped many a cart wheel, using a circular stone and a carefully controlled fire to heat up the circlet of iron which was then adroitly slipped over the wooden wheel and cooled so that it contracted and held the wheel in a vice-like grip.

His successor as blacksmith was David Tuke, the Tosside smith, who periodically visited Stocks and had achieved the rare distinction in competition of being judged the best blacksmith in the country. "He was a good blacksmith but he had one fault—he used to nail t'shoes on too tight. We used to tell him about it. . . Eventually, he and his lads—Titch and Tommy—went to Oswaldtwistle."

The Tosside enterprise was taken over by Bob and John Rawsthorne, of Gisburn, though a Dalehead farmer who had patronised Mr Tuke at Tosside began to go to Fred Hayhurst, of Holden. A tiny smithy existed at Hesbert Hall, which was then a group of three farms with outbuildings.

Reading Room

Completing the range of facilities at Stocks Fold was the Reading Room, which stood at the top of a flight of stone steps in the L-shaped block which held the shop and the smithy. "Men gathered at the Reading Room to cal [gossip]. There wasn't a billiards table or anything."

During the 1914-18 war, this room "up t'steps" became a furniture repository. The furniture belonged to Heber and Fanny Carr of Wigglesworth. When war broke out, and he joined the Army, he arranged for his wife and their infant child to return to Bridge House, her parents' home. The family belongings were put in store for the duration.

The Farms

You'd hardly credit it, but nearly all these little farms supported big families. They had a pretty hard time of it, no doubt, working hard under poorish conditions, but on the whole they were contented and healthy enough.

John Walmsley (1957).

The farmers were poor by today's standards, but friendly and helpful to each other—more like one big family.

Tom Cowking.

A provender chap came from Waddington once a month. He said something that was not very nice about one of the Dalehead families. My father said: "Thee bi careful what tha's talking about. They're related to me."

There was no spare time in summer. We were farming for 18 years and never had a holiday.

Doris Wells.

There'd been a Robinson for years at Stephen Park. Our landlord, Billy Procter, of Kirkby Malham, once said that as as long as a Robinson was left the family had to have the farm...

Vic Robinson, Clitheroe Advertiser (1991).

AT DALEHEAD, before the Flood, lived a tough and self-reliant farming community. The farms were squandered [scattered] down the valley and on the slopes of the flanking hills. The horizons were low. The big sky often filled with rain clouds, for Bowland is one of the wettest areas in England.

The largest farms, Lamb Hill and Catlow, were spoken of with awe by the tenants of places of modest size, where there were a few sheep and fewer cows. A good average for a local farm was 30 acres of inland [meadow and good pasture] with about 16 cattle.

38

All the Dalehead farms had to support large families.

A farmer aimed to sell four cows a year, having raised them from calves. The income from those four cows paid the rent—and left "a bit over". The farm had a few sheep, one or two pigs and some poultry.

New House, Hasgill, Birch Hill, Chapel House—the farms were spread along the flanks of the fells, with one or two near the Hodder.

Halsteads, Swinshaw, Greenfold, Hesbert Hall—they had attractive names with the ring of antiquity.

Stephen Park, Black House, Clough (pronounced "cloo") and Hollins—the names fall from the lips of Daleheaders as though from a litany.

Churning for Butter

At the turn of the century, the cattle were milked by hand, twice a day, in tiny shippons flavoured by the smell of hay and dung. None of the milk left the farms as milk. That which was not required for household use was skimmed, the cream being made into butter and what remained—the "blue" milk—being fed to the young stock or the pigs.

A familiar sound in every farm kitchen was the rumble of the end-to-end churn, where cream was converted into butter.

It was a tedious job, especially in summer, when the cream was slow to turn. The speed at which the churn was spun was important. "If you were going too fast, it was not making butter. You had to slacken t'speed off till you could hear it splashing t'sides again or you'd never have finished."

If a "round pound" was made, a butter stamp of sycamore gave the product of a farm a distinctive appearance, one stamp featuring a thistle, another a cow and yet another a rose. A farmer's wife told me: "I bet them stamps are worth something now."

Hen eggs retailed at a shilling per dozen. When the pigs were killed, the farmer kept the poorer cuts for his household and sold the best meat.

Off for the Day

Some of the little farms of Dalehead were so remote that a Clitheroe tradesman, arriving one Easter, was invited to "let in" the New Year. Doris Wells, who was brought up at Halsteads, to which the family moved in 1910, recalls that twice a year her mother went to Settle to get some new clothes or shoes for her children.

It was a journey undertaken on foot with mother crossing the ridge to the north of Whelpstone Crag and descending Giggleswick Common to Sandford and Wham. "You never heard farmers talk about money but I remember that for a trip to Settle mother was given a blank cheque."

It was a special treat to go to Morecambe. Mother took her family—and any number of neighbours' children—to Clapham railway station by horse and float. It was exciting to cross the ridge at Bowland Knotts and see ahead the lion-like form of Ingleborough.

Doris, who acquired an aunt's bike when she left school, cycled to Clapham station. "The road was like any other country road—a cart track! It was grand going down from Bowland Knotts. We won't say anything about coming back."

The horse was stabled at the *Flying Horseshoe*. More often than not it was dusk or even dark when they returned over Bowland Knotts, following the white ribbon of the unmetalled road and hoping to remain on it.

Dalehead School and the adjacent Headmaster's house.

Above: A fine stallion outside Stephen Park. *Below:* View of Bottoms Farm.

Above: Grange Hall, the home of the Cowking family, stood on the site of property owned by Kirkstall Abbey. *Below:* The Church Army caravan, parked at Dalehead for a brief evangelistic campaign.

Above: A general view of Dalehead from near the Low Barn, Grange Hall. The trees (right) stand beside the river Hodder. *Below:* The New Inn, Dalehead, owned by T G Robinson. It was bought by John Swale and re-named The Travellers' Rest.

Above: The Vicarage at Dalehead, viewed from the extensive grounds. *Below:* Dalehead Church, which was re-built in a shorter form at a site well above high water level. *Opposite page:* Dalehead School (centre) with the Headmaster's house above and an interior of the School below.

Above: J Swale's joinery business at Dalehead. He later purchased the local inn.
Below: A car owned by Mr Killick, the Headmaster, who once took a party of children in two cars to Morecambe.

Above: A group at the opening ceremony at Stocks reservoir, 1932. On the right is Prince George (later Duke of Kent). *Below:* The dam under construction.

Two groups photographed at Hollins, the shanty village of the construction period.
Above: H Cottam (resident engineer), sixth from the left, and the office staff.
Below: The cinema at Hollins village on the occasion of a potato pie supper marking
the completion of the tunnel at the dam.

The Farmstock

The Dalehead farmers ran their sheep on moors which in those days held a lot of heather, glowing wine-red during the flowering season of late autumn when the gentry had a few days grouse-shooting. Farmers tried to keep some life in their jaded acres by applying muck from the shippons or occasionally lime from one of the handiest field kilns.

These men were outstanding with stock but had among them specialists, such as Stephen Robinson, who had a name for dealing with ruptures in foals. Bob Parker, who lived at Colleyholme, was skilled at attending to sturdy, a complaint of sheep caused by tapeworms from the droppings from a stray dog or from rabbits, if they were numerous.

A sheep with sturdy "went round in a circle, ten or a dozen yards for a start and eventually following its tail. In wet weather t'ground was absolutely puddled up." When the sturdy was ripe, Bob felt the front of the sheep's skull, looking for the place where the parasite had become lodged. This area went "as soft as putty, about size of half a crown."

Bob drove a hole into the skull to recover "a bladder full of water and seeds. It's about t'size of a water-blether [bladder] out of a rabbit." The wound was then dressed but the sheep was "niv-ver reight after. They always ended up drowning, or something."

In the pre-cattle wagon age, when the handiest marketing centre for Dalehead stock was Hellifield, farmers took their animals to join a drove organised by Mr Carr. This drove left Slaidburn on Wednesday morning, arriving at the Tosside-Slaidburn crossroads near Stoney Bank at about 9 a.m.

The farmers paid the drovers a small fee. Tom Cowking recalls that as most of the cattle had not been away from home before, it was sometimes quite an effort to be on time at the meeting point.

At Hellifield, cattle were penned overnight and, fed and watered, were in good condition for the Thursday sale, while still showing the stress of rough handling by dogs and the rigours of the road. The owners travelled to Hellifield independently, on horseback or by horse and trap, to sell their stock. If they wished Mr Carr to put a batch of cattle through the ring for them, they paid him half-a-crown.

The Dalehead sheep drank in a love of the home acres with their mothers' milk and most of them had no inclination to stray. The footloose aninmals, known as "strags", were returned to their rightful owners at gathering-time.

Hired Help

The farmfolk, like the sheep, were disinclined to wander away from Dalehead. Some of them were born, lived, loved and died within the bounds of the Bowland fells. There was an infusion of new life by way of the hirings for farm servants.

A young man or girl, taken on at the hirings, either locally or at Ulverston and other places on the Cumbrian coast, worked for six months at the discretion of the employer (which often meant long hours of hard labour) for a pittance. Board and lodging were provided.

Arguably, the young man was learning about farming and the young woman, who was employed mainly in the house, was being taught housewifery. To most farmers, the hired servant represented cheap labour.

At many a farm, early this century, the family sat at one table and the farm men occupied another. Yet cases were known of farm men marrying the farmers' daughters. The little servant lass from Ulverston, growing up into womanhood, might become the wife of a farmer's son.

Mrs Tillotson, a farmer's daughter, was fond of recalling the days when it was considered a crime for a woman to smoke or drink. The lads would not dare to smoke tobacco in front of their fathers.

Well-brought-up young ladies never used make-up or plaited their hair until early this century, when the strict code was relaxed. Mrs Tillotson remembered turning her hair round clothes pegs which were left up all night to encourage the hair to curl. It was not conducive to a good night's sleep.

Everyday Footwear

Clogs were a common form of footwear, for children attending school and also for farmers and their men clumping about their daily work. Clogs raised the feet above the damp ground and turned snow-broth (the mush as snow melted). In snowtime, the wearer was constantly kicking away the clods that built up beneath the soles.

George Robinson, when in his late teens, made hundreds of pairs of clogs at Catlow. He cut the soles from alder wood which had grown on the farm. Or he would buy some ready-made clogs for handiness.

"I used to make my own uppers as well. I was taught by an Irishman we had for two or three years. He had been a shoemaker in America. So I used to make my own patterns and everything."

A girl's clog had one bar or a clasp. Boys usually had clogs that laced up. Clogs made for a child were tidy and light. "I have made clogs—uppers and soles—for as cheap as 5s.6d a pair."

By and large, the Dalehead farmers were well disposed towards their families and their men but, as in every community, there were those who squandered their money on drink. A man who went to the pub virtually every night kept his wife and family so short of money she had to take in washing. When the two oldest lads grew up, they turned on father and "brayed him up one neet. It did him a lot o' good."

Tea (which John Wesley had denounced as a wicked drug from the Orient) was little known on Dalehead farms. At mealtimes, the farmers drank milk or home-brewed beer.Tom Cowking says: "Two of my aunts got to going to places where tea was served. They developed a liking for it. Eventually we had tea with our meals."

Lamb Hill Clipping

Dalehead was split among several landowners, one of whom was Col Hirst, "a tremendous big, stiff man", who was a textile magnate as well as the owner of Croasdale and Lamb Hill. It is recalled that the Greenwood brothers, Jack and Joe, were among the last hinds to be employed by this wealthy man who was "a sporty chap—what you would call a gentleman."

The Colonel maintained a close interest in his farms. At Lamb Hill (farmed by William Cowking) the activity most keenly anticipated was the sheep-clipping, when hundreds of sheep were robbed of their fleeces in a single day. The routine was unchanging and exhausting.

For every clipper there was a sheep-catcher and a sheep-marker. In the background, too, were the women, wearing well-starched aprons, keeping up the supply of food and drink, including beer. "The clippers got a bit market-fresh as the day went on."

School lads, playing truant, did the sheep-catching, being paid three shillings a day. When they returned to school, they were whacked for being absent from their lessons. Experienced men did the clipping (with hand-shears, of course). Others rolled up the fleeces, securing each with a loosely twisted piece of wool.

When the clipping was over, everyone went to the house for a substantial meal of roast beef, potatoes and peas, with pudding and cake to follow. Those who wished danced away the night, returning to their homes as the eastern sky pearled with the approach of a new day.

An Outpost of Kirkstall

Grange Hall, established when the de Lacys gave land and animals to Kirkstall Abbey, was the most venerable farm. The area was previously known as Rushton. Local tradition claims that the stables at Grange Hall were originally a chapel. There was also talk of a secret room, entered by a sliding panel, and of space near a chimney with a row of hooks, presumably for smoking beef or mutton.

At the front of Grange Hall was a stone pillar surmounted by a stone ball about which there was much speculation, some people suggesting it was to mark a burial place. It was one of the grinding stones from a small corn mill.

The Cowking family had been associated with Grange Farm since early in the 17th century. It was then farmed by Thomas Cowking (born 1823) who also farmed New Close. When two maiden aunts, Betty and Bertha, presided over Grange Hall the staff consisted of two regular men, plus four Irishmen hired for a month at haytime. The main Cowking family was settled at New Close and the two farms were worked together.

Tom Cowking's father married Miss M J Carter, from the New Inn at Dalehead, and took her to New Close, which they farmed until father's death in exceptional circumstances—internal injuries caused when helping to move a particularly wild bull to Slaidburn.

He was feeling unwell when he went to bed that night. The doctor was called but no improvement was noticed. A nurse was engaged and medicines brought from Settle and Clitheroe. Poppy heads were boiled to extract the opium. Morphia tablets were crushed into powder with a flat iron but nothing seemed to ease the pain.

Father was dead within a week and mother had to continue farming New Close and attend to her five children.

Latterly, Dalehead depended on the doctor at Slaidburn. Tom

Cowking recalls that in the absence of a telephone at Dalehead post office, if there was sickness at New Close the doctor arrived in the horse and trap and Tom then returned with him to Slaidburn to collect any medicine which had been prescribed.

About 1918-19, a temporary man who was helping out at New Close in haytime had toothache. He was taken to the doctor at Slaidburn by horse and trap. The offending tooth was extracted in the doctor's garden and a charge of half a crown was made.

Haytime Meals

Ivy Waddington, who spent her childhood at Bridge House, with her mother and grandparents, William and Jane Hanson, told me of the day when she and her cousin, Harold, were sent to the meadow with drinkings (haytime refreshment). They were expressly asked to return with the dirty mugs.

Harold, who was holding the bag, grew so weary he dropped them and the mugs broke. He pushed them behind a bush and, on his return to the farm, said the mugs must have been left in the hayfield.

The story held up until the autumn leaf fall, when the bush lost its leaves and the the the broken crockery came to view. As Ivy says: "It gave the show away."

In the Larder

The Tillotsons of Fair Hill were a large family—mother, father, eight girls and six boys. We know a little about them because Mrs R Tillotson, who was born in 1887, was persuaded to talk about the old days. She recalled the type of food they ate.

Each month, they ordered from a Settle grocer 28 lb of lard, 14 lb of currants and 1 cwt of sugar. Mrs Tillotson's mother made 18 pies and pasties which lasted for two days. On baking day, she had up to 10 loaves in the oven at once, hence the need for 70 lb of flour a week.

Every fortnight, mother turned to making oatcakes, 100 at a time, each a yard long and dried on a rack near the fire until it had become crisp and resembled a wash leather. Oatcake was made more palatable by being eaten with butter and cheese, both local products.

The Carrs

At Fair Hill, in 1909, the Carr family—parents and their 14 children—assembled for a photograph; it was the Sunday after Stocks Sports and the only occasion on which the family was together at one time.

When Heber Carr was called up into the Royal Engineers, in 1914, his wife took her infant daughter Ivy to her family home, Bridge House, and here they stayed throughout the war. It claimed the lives of Jack and Willie Carr, two brothers who were slain within a fortnight of each other.

There were Carrs at White Hill House, a holding of some 50 acres beside the road leading to Bowland Knotts. The first of the Carrs to own it was William, who hailed from Whitendale, but—as was the way with many properties when big families was the rule—at his death it was divided among a number of descendants. One of his sons, Thomas Carr, paid rent for it.

The old Dalehead families did not go far for their mates. Thomas Carr courted and won Jane Harrison, of Wham. And, says their eldest daughter, Doris, "my mother's mother was a Frankland from New Hall."

Leaving the Groceries

Doris also tells about Till Robinson ("my Grandmother Carr's brother"), who lived at Swinshaw, where there was a large cart house. When Shepherd and Walker from Settle and others had motor transport, they left goods at the shed on a Thursday to meet orders that were previously handed in. Farmers, when collecting these items, left butter and eggs to be collected by those who dealt in such commodities.

"I remember when Claytons, the grocers at Settle, left stuff at Swinshaw. They wrapped their groceries in strong brown paper—lovely paper—tied with yards of string. Fairhurst, the butcher at Long Preston, used the cart shed at Swinshaw. You placed your order one week and he delivered it on the following week."

Near Whelpstone Crag

Some of the most remote farms, high up near Whelpstone Crag and Holden Moor, were approached from Tosside, using Bailey Lane. Robin Waddington, who was brought up in those parts recalls when Whelpstone Crag and Holden Moor were covered with ling and had a stock of grouse.

Northfield, a farm nestling at the foot of Whelpstone, was home to the Lodge family. The children went to Dalehead School, to and fro, on foot, a daily round of some eight miles.

The Misses Taylor—Dolly, Grace and Violet—of Hensley Hill entertained local people with their antics, which included taking a cow to a neighbour's bull at night without him being aware of it. These ladies, buying a nine gallon barrel of beer, had it delivered to Wham Farm, from which they wheeled it up and over Whelpstone Crag to their home, negotiating several walls en route.

Not far away stood Owlshaw, to which the farmer summoned Manserghs of Rathmell to do some joinery work. Robin Waddington and Edward Lamb were the workmen. They cycled to Owlshaw and were invited indoors to have their packed meal.

Robin had put his bicycle in a shippon but Edward left his outdoors. They heard a crashing sound. "A horse was stamping on

Edward's bike, as much as to say: 'I'll flatten you'. We clubbed up at t'mill to buy Edward a fresh bike."

Robinsons at Stephen Park

Stephen Park, a 17th century building (1662) was the home of generations of Robinsons. Stephen and Susannah had six children, the eldest being Drina. Vic Robinson, a brother, told me that there was "a bit of a mix-up" when she was christened. Mother wanted her to be called Alexandria. The vicar said "Alexandrina." So they left it at that.

Stephen Park, which belonged to William Procter of Winterburn, had an acreage of 400. Over the main doorway (which was eventually obscured by a porch and thus formed the door to the parlour) was inscribed: "He that doth passe must honest be. Not too bold for you see. HMB 1662."

Vic recalls Stephen Park as a bad spot for farming. "It was boggy and not good for sheep." In the 1930s, the Fylde Water Board put the two Greenfolds to it. "That did it. You could tell by the stock. If you ever wanted your milk cows they would be on the Greenfolds."

Stephen Park was a busy farm, with four servant men. Those recalled by Vic are Charlie Seed, Major Seed, Jim Seed and George Pollard. The farmhouse was "a cold spot" and each summer a month was devoted to peat-digging, which kept the old place warm. "We used to fill the turf-house up to the beam, like a mewstead [hay stored in a barn]."

The kitchen, "a big roaming place", had a backstone [literally stone, not a metal plate, with a fire beneath for making oatcakes]. The oatmeal was prepared the day before baking day. Mother used a large round dish [from Burton-in-Lonsdale pottery]. She had an early start, produced a lot of oatcake and put it on the clothes rack to dry.

Oatcakes were eaten with butter and, sometimes, Lyle's golden syrup. "We bought the syrup in a drum the size of a petrol can. Many a time we had oatcakes for breakfast in place of porridge and we put milk on it."

Grange Hall Farm.

Through The Year

THE Dalehead winter was long and usually hard. In 1917 it had a sting in its tail. Doris Wells, who was living at Halsteads at that time, recalls: "We had a severe snowstorm in March and then a hard frost, so it was possible for us to walk over the walls on our way to school.

"In April, when lambing began, the snow and ice were still there. The sheep could not reach the grass and had to be fed on what was left of the hay. The milk given by the cows was poured into basins and given to the ewes to drink.

"That year, it was not until the end of April that the thaw got under way. I remember being at school when my father went past, driving some of his sheep to the bottom fields, which were greening up."

Altogether, 1917 was a miserable year. The war was still raging. Two of Doris's uncles died while on military service in France.

Sheep in the Snow

Vic Robinson has special memories of winter weather in 1936, when a blizzard "took us unawares. We were six weeks without bread. We lived on scones, having plenty of flour but no yeast. When we got a supply of bread it tasted really good."

He went looking for overblown sheep "beyond the two Greenfolds, which the Fylde Water Board had added to Stephen Park. It was the best sheep land." A hundred sheep, sheltering from the blizzard, had got at the back of a thorn fence for shelter and they "landed up in a gully-hole fourteen to sixteen feet deep." Vic, single-handed, managed to rescue about 60 sheep.

The victims were mainly the hoggs (last year's lambs) which, being the smallest and weakest, were at the bottom and drowned. Sometimes, he made a great effort to get a sheep to safety only to see it totter back into the hole. The strain on the man was considerable. "I was done for by the time I got 'em out."

At Dalehead, in a normal year, snow fell after Christmas and the worst of winter weather began with snow carried on an easterly. Snow which arrived from that direction was in no hurry to melt. By mid-February, a hill farmer was keen to have at least half of his hay crop left.

Winter was enlivened for the young folk by dances. Not many were held. George Robinson was one of those who travelled on horseback to various dances. One evening he crossed the ridge to dance in a wooden hut at Bentham. There was another such hut at Eldroth, near Austwick.

Tewit Eggs

When a cock lapwing was seen tumbling and calling over the pastures, it was a good indication that the tardy Bowland spring was at hand. Farm lads scoured the district for the eggs of the lapwing (known locally as tewit, after its call).

These eggs were sold to a Mr Clark of Settle, who—after testing them, and rejecting any that floated—sent them to the top hotels in London. The price in March was sixpence. As eggs became more plentiful, it fell to a penny, or even less.

Soon the contralto bleating of the hill ewes was joined by the soprano calls of new lambs.

When, in due season, the wool crop was taken by horse and cart to a warehouse at Long Preston, the cart was laden with coal for the return trip. Children were delighted when such journeys were held on a Saturday, when they did not have to go to school.

Cart Loads of Coal

Tom Cowking recalls that the horses were baited (fed) at the Plough Inn, Wigglesworth, and as several farmers had agreed to deliver their wool on the same day, calling at the *Plough* could end in quite a party!

He remembers that when one farmer "went off his legs" after a few drinks, his friends lifted him on to his load of coal. This meant that another man had to take two carts—a rather difficult task as a "trace horse" was used up the hills.

When Tom was in his teens, he was allowed to go on his own to pick up a load of coal at Chatburn, stopping for food at the *Spread Eagle,* Sawley, which then was a small country inn kept by Mr J Speak. He was well-known to the Cowking family, from whom he bought pig hams for his catering trade.

At the *Spread Eagle,* Tom was provided with a large plate of beef and ham with trimmings, followed by a wedge of slab-cake and a pint of tea, plus food for the horse—and all for two shillings.

Most of the Dalehead mums were good cooks. Tom relates that the hot air oven at Grange Hall was set high on the wall, with three dampers. In it were cooked potato pies and pasties. The staple meats were beef, mutton and bacon, all capable of being produced on the home farm.

Sheep Washing

A short time before sheep-clipping, the animals were washed, to remove traces of sand and peat from the moors. Washing also removed the last traces of the salve which had been spread on the skins of the sheep in November.

At Grange Hall, for the washing, the river Hodder was dammed, creating a deep pool. The sheep stepped into it from a launching platform which consisted of barn doors taken from their hinges for the occasion. One man dropped a sheep into the dub, where another man ruffled the wool. Traces of salve, entering the water, stupefied the fish, which could be readily caught.

In early summer, if there was a freshet in the river, Tom Cowking went with his father to fish for trout with rod and line.

Peat-cutting

June was the month when conical heaps appeared at peaty places on the fells. Each heap was composed of turves of peat, cut with the help of a special winged spade and transported to the drying area on a special low-slung barrow which had a large wheel.

The peats were reared up to be dried by wind and sunshine, then put into the conical heaps. The drying process continued until, in good weather, they might be carted down to the farm, some to be stored in a peat house and others made into a stack at the gable end.

Doris Wells says: "We didn't burn any coal at Halsteads Farm, though it was because of coal that we got there. The farmer—they called him Paler—was killed while carting a load of coal from Clapham station. He'd got over Bowland Knotts and was coming down Crutchenber when he sat on a shaft so that he could brake the cart. He slipped off and a wheel went over him.

"At Halsteads, we had a coal house. There were two big lumps of coal in it when we arrived—and the same two big lumps were there when we moved to Martin Top 15 years later!

A peat fire rarely went out. In the morning, there was a glow from the embers of yesterday's fire. The Tillotsons of Fair Hill did not use a cob of coal for 30 years because each summer peat was cut and 80 cart loads were stacked by the house.

Doris recalls life at Halsteads, from which peat-digging expeditions took place each summer. "If we were going to school, we had to help out on Saturday, laying out the peats to dry—one propped against another, with a third peat balanced on top. If there was a wind, it was a dusty job.

"On a Saturday, when we were off school, mother made up the drinkings [outdoor snack] and we youngsters would take it up to where the men were working. There were no sandwiches—just chunks of bread and butter, with perhaps some jam pasty. The drink itself was cold tea in a can."

If it was a good drying summer—"we seemed to get a lot better summers then, you know"—we could take a few loads down to the farm in good time and cart the rest later. We had a peat-house and also stacked peat in part of a granary.

Sometimes, there was so much peat, we put what was left under a sort of lean-to to keep the weather off it."

Catlow got its peat from New House Fell. "There were turf-pits on Catlow Fell but New House was handier."

Vic Robinson, who was reared at Stephen Park, dug peat at a deep pit on the high ground between the farm and Tosside. The peat came out as dark and hard as coal. "On a right hot day, we'd nothing to shelter us. You couldn't get out of t'way of t'sun. You'd to grin and bear it.

"We started off with two barrows. My brother used to get the turf and put it on the barrows. We had to wheel it out and tip it. When we covered all t'ground, we reared it up, one against another, so that grass would grow in between. Grass wouldn't have let it dry.

"It was a back-aching job. You couldn't kneel down on that sort of land. There was quite a lot of work with it. When one side got dry, we turned it and then we put it into 'honeycombs' [conical heaps, with spaces to admit the air]."

The peat was transported back to Stephen Park by horse and cart. The cart had shelvings, often pronounced "shilvings" [a wooden extension frame].

The Big Clippings

Sheep-clippings at Lamb Hill and Catlow were on such a large scale they have become the stuff of legends. Tom Cowking relates that "the men who helped clipped all day and danced all night." Doris Wells, commenting on a photograph of the Lamb Hill clipping of 1906, and what her mother had told her, said it was an important enough event for mother to make a blouse especially for it. She also attended wearing a well-laundered skirt and a long white overall.

The round of various farms, as recalled by Vic Robinson, began with the stock of John Holland at Crutchenber. "We clipped his sheep and then went to Dick Wallbank's at Halsteads and clipped there, followed by Charlie Robinson's [at the other Halsteads Farm], and two days clipping for the Robinsons at Hesbert Hall. The men then had two days with the Robinsons at Catlow. "By this time, we really could clip. We'd had plenty of practice!"

Butter Production

George Robinson, as a young man at Catlow, made about 70 lb of butter a week. The cows were milked by hand and the milk poured into large shallow vats known as "leads" because at one time they were made of lead. Here the milk stood for "three meals" or "three milkings".

The "leads" reposed on stone slabs which had holes at intervals, these coinciding with the plug of a vat. When a plug was removed, the "blue" milk was drawn off into a bucket, to be fed to the calves, leaving the cream to be gently scraped off the "lead" and placed in a crock for the making of butter.

In summer, it was known for the contents of a churn to "go to sleep", reaching a certain stage when it went stiff and remained in one end of the churn. "It wasn't moving," comments George Robinson. "I remember this happening when we had an Irish haytime man. He said he would cure it and told me to add a dessert spoonful of vinegar, which I did. It worked. The acid just cracked it."

Early this century, butter was retailing at less than a shilling a pound. It was the time when you might buy a score of eggs for tenpence. Hens did not cost much to keep, however, for a farmer could buy their main food, split corn, for 2s.9d a hundredweight.

Making Hay

Betty and Bertha Cowking, at Grange Hall, were among those who brewed ale when the labour force was about to be enlarged by the appearance of four Irish haytime workers. They stayed a month for a fixed sum, with board and lodging provided.

The two ladies had a special treat before haytime—a day off in Clitheroe, travelling the 11 miles by a trap drawn by Bonny, the little chestnut mare, specially groomed by Billie Parker, her mane and tail bedecked with coloured ribbons.

Bonny hauled them over the rough road, across the Hodder ford near Grange Hall and off to town, where they bought household necessities, excepting food, which were required over the next six months.

At the approach of the hay season, barns were cleaned up. Each barn was unique in its size and appearance. Dog Wark Barn had a name relating to a wager struck between two men, one betting the other that he could not mow by scythe the meadow adjoining the barn—in a single day.

The bet was accepted. The scythesman went to work and as the long hours passed he seemed to have the task well in hand. It was suspected that he had taken a stimulant with his food and drink. He completed the work minus his trousers. The effort of mowing the field proved too much for him. He died that same night.

The Irish haytime men, many of them from County Mayo, made

directly for the farms where they had been employed before, and where their return was welcomed, or they attended a hiring fair, such as that held at Bentham in late June (the men were called "June barbers"). Others congregated at Gisburn and Bolton-by-Bowland.

A deal between a farmer and an Irishman was made. The actual pay was about £4 for the month, with the proviso that if the hay was in before the month was up, the Irishman was free to go elsewhere with full pay. The bargain was sealed with a handclasp and the farmer handed over a shilling.

The Irishmen professed ignorance of any other farm task except hay-making. On Sunday, when haymaking was in abeyance, the workers from Old Oireland, clad in blue suits, with brown boots, which was almost a uniform, set off from the farms to attend Mass at Dunsop Bridge. Copy Nook was their favourite pub.

Irishmen who gathered at Grange Hall on Sundays sat in a circle and one of them, called Martin, told them stories of their homeland. If the local children crept near to listen to what was being said, Martin would instantly switch to speaking his native Irish. Far from discouraging the children, this made them more than ever interested in what was happening. They had previously heard no other language but English.

At Dalehead, in the early part of this century, haytime was basically a hand operation, with no strawing [strewing-out] or side-delivery machines. Mowing machines were uncommon enough to excite comment.

The Dalehead blacksmith and the joiner busied themselves, the latter repairing cart shelvings, repairing or supplying hay rakes and attending to the horse-drawn sleds which moved as easily over the springy summer turf as they would on winter snow.

Tom Cowking remembers seeing a team of six men with scythes working in unison in a Dalehead meadow. The blades made a conspicuous swishing sound as they swept through the grass. Each was capable of cutting a swathe from five to six feet wide. In good weather, one of Tom's uncles rose from his bed at 4 a.m. to mow with a scythe. He breakfasted on porridge, whey and fatcakes.

The men were well-fed to keep up their strength. At lunchtime, there was hung-beef (bull beef, cut into strips and dried) plus potatoes. The beef was soaked to reconstitute it before cooking. "Uncle did not recommend it!"

Hardly anyone drank tea. They slaked their thirst with milk, whey or home brewed ale. (When the men were out for bracken or peat, they took with them ale in a gallon bottle, held in a wicker basket. It was attached to the cart shelving for the journey to the fell).

At Grange Hall, when tea became more popular, beer was being served at two meals in the day. And, of course, a copious quantity was made for quenching haytime thirsts. Tom Cowking recalls: "I was bottle-carrier. And sometimes I was a bit dizzy when I got to the hayfield."

Irish Haytimers

The like of these Irish workers is never seen today. They came from primitive homes where humans and livestock shared a common roof. They wore heavy clothing, mufflers and long johns. At Grange Hall, they slept in an adjoining building. "My aunt dreaded making up their beds and she used a matchbox to catch the jumpers (fleas)."

Mrs George Robinson remembers when an Irishman hired for Bridge House did hardly any work. "He broke down with measles and was very bad."

In haytime, at Grange and Hammerton Halls, the food included sheep, killed at the rate of one a week alternately between the two places. A sheep carcass was deftly split into two and half taken to the other farm. So once a fortnight, Tom Cowking carried a piece of mutton the two miles from Grange Hall to Hammerton Hall. A week later, it was the turn of his cousin Cyril to do the same in the reverse direction.

A large shell was blown to summon the men to dinner at the Grange. Blowing it was a special knack which only Aunt Bertha and one of the men could manage. The sound (recalls Tom) seemed to echo round the valley and could be heard by people living a mile away.

When the hay was dry and fit for leading, it was put into rows and the ground raked clean, for nothing must be wasted. The laden cart had to be kemmed [combed, or raked down] before it left the field.

Repairs to the Road

Summertime saw the patching of the waterbound roads with a mixture of stones and soil, well watered. A waterbound road soon had potholes which were traps for unwary cyclists, who frequently had punctures when riding over Bowland Knotts or by the Cross o' Greet.

Local farmers on contract did much of the carrying. One of them provided a horse which was yoked to the water cart. Others transported stones and soil. Tom Cowking recalls that he ran up to a mile from school to see a steam roller at work. A driver who had a young audience thrilled the children by giving a few toots on the steam whistle or blowing jets of steam towards them.

The summer sunshine and breezes dried off the turves of peat which had been cut as fuel for the domestic fire. The area near Bowland Knotts was a famous peat-ground. Tom Cowking recalls when two men worked in unison, one standing at the top of the pit, giving a downward cut to create a "peat" which then was severed from the hagg by a forward movement on the part of the second man, who stood in the pit itself. This man also lifted it on to the flat, sideless barrow.

Bracken for Bedding

As the bracken withered on the fells, farmers with horses and sleds scythed the bronze-tinted fronds and bundled them for transportation to the road, thence by horse and cart to the farm-yards, where they were stacked to provide bedding for the over-wintering stock. The clegs brought down in the bracken were a trial to horses in winter before these insect pests died off.

Sieves (rushes) were also scythed and carted as bedding. Doris Wells recalls: "I was helping my dad to get some rushes, and was raking them from beside a wall, when I saw something moving in the wall. I called dad. He said I must come away—it was a stoat. He didn't know how many other stoats there might be, and it was best to ignore them. If I saw a stoat after that, I felt queezy."

The Sportsmen

Grouse shooting in late summer and autumn brought some "nobs" to the district. The Hirst family had sporting rights over most of the ground in and around the Hodder basin. George Robinson remembers Jules Hirst, who was half-Hungarian.

One of the first cars seen at Dalehead, prior to the 1914-18 war, was owned by this family. The vehicle was a chauffeur-driven Hodgkiss, "a Hungarian car, of course," it was "more like a charabanc than a car."

Col Hirst, a well-built type and "a real nice chap—a proper gentleman", had his main home in Renfrewshire and rented Town Head, Slaidburn, during the shooting season. The colonel brought his domestic staff with him. His daughters, Miss Diana and Miss Prudence, were to be seen about the district. Col Hirst's son eventually emigrated to Australia.

The game was varied and numerous, including both black and red grouse, pheasant, partridge and hare. Col Hirst did not object to local lads catching rabbits.

The colonel had a Rolls Royce and Mercedes, which he used for transporting shooters and essential supplies from his summer headquarters at Slaidburn to the selected moor. Tom Cowking says that the jovial chauffeurs sometimes gave children a ride in these posh vehicles. "I suppose they got a kick from our reaction to having our first car ride."

Grouse were under fire from August 12. The sportsmen dined well on food taken to the shooting box on horseback. The farmer at Lamb Hill supplied one sheep a week during the season, this being taken to Town Head by one of the chauffeurs to help feed the large staff.

Elsewhere, rough shooting was practised. A Daleheader recalls: "I went beating for a chap but I fell out wi' him. It was against Bowland Knotts. He had me loadened up. He kept shooting hares and handing them over for me to carry. I think I had three hares, or four, and—you know—and they weighed summat.

"I already had a big bag of cartridges on my back and a spare gun. What the devil he wanted a spare gun for, I don't know. He shot a grouse on New House Fell. He gave me that and then he wanted me to go right round outside o' t'moor and drive 'em in to me. I said: 'What have I got to do with all this stuff?' He said: 'Take them with you.' I dropped it—and went home.

"It was one Saturday—I'll never forget. It was only about ten shillings for t'day. Father said I shouldn't have left. I said: 'Blow him, he wanted me to go with him. I didn't bargain for that so I cleared."

It was in autumn that Dalehead farmers went off to Hawes, Kirkby Stephen—even, at times, to Barnard Castle—to obtain their rams for the tupping season which was imminent. It was vital to introduce "fresh blood" into the flocks to avoid in-breeding.

Sheep Salving

Another job to fit in before the onset of winter was sheep-salving. Tom Cowking recalls that the salve applied to the skins of the sheep was a mixture of Stockholm tar and grease, spread with the finger after the wool had been shedded (parted in strips).

"This was a very tedious job for the farmer and on a big sheep farm it took weeks. The object of applying grease was to 'water-proof' the animals. They 'wintered' better if they were salved. Nowadays, dipping is the only special preparation for the winter."

George Robinson recalls: "It was mainly fell sheep we salved, to protect them from the weather." He helped to mix salve, using white tar, black Stockholm tar (bought from Sedgwicks of Sedbergh), brown grease, old butter (from butter merchants, to make the salve run easier), candle fat (common in those pre-electric days) and a bit o' butter milk to take t'fire out of it.

The farmfolk also blithely handled a deadly poison, known to them as "hallibore", which was added to kill the ticks (parasites). "Hallibore" was obtained in powder form from Shepherd and Walker at Settle, who were well-established chemists.

The tar and grease were purchased in either three and a-half hundredweight or four hundredweight barrels. "We got a cross-cut saw and sawed a barrel straight through the middle. Then we'd two tubs.

"On a wet cold day we'd be on making salve in t'granary, where there was a place to light a big fire. We mixed salve in a pan that could be swung round over t'fire like a reckon. When you wanted to lift a pan off, you swizzled t'reckon round.

"We had a spade like a garden spade and kept sticking it into t'fire. When it was right hot we could use it to cut into the tar, which was hard. We could then put in into t'pan, with so many panfuls of each into one of these half-barrels. Then we had to stir the buttermilk into the grease and tar. It was quite a job because they were not too keen to mix. They eventually worked in.

"When you had your ingredients all in together you'd put this powder in. It was about the only thing that would kill ticks in those days. For salving, nobody wore gloves. A salver had a big thick sack round his waist. It was tied wi' string at t'back. I've been afire above once! I'd roll on t'floor to put the fire out."

The salvers frequently had to work at night in a stuffy, smelly atmosphere. "Salve had a smell of its own," says George, who then relates how it was applied. "You had your big vat and then you had your salving bowl, which had a long handle underneath and a bolt in at t'bottom to fasten it on. The old sheep stock [a sort of form with room for man and one sheep] had holes at the side into which you stuck a salving pan.

"You shed [parted in rows] your sheep wool and used a finger to stroke some tar on to the sheep's skin you had bared. A 'shedding' would be roughly one and a-half inches apart. "I never got to salving properly. My job was to sit on a milking stool with a little pan aside of me, doing tails.

"At that time there were no more than 200 sheep at Catlow. It took about three-quarters of an hour to salve a sheep. We used to hire men for salving at that time for from six to eight weeks."

Winter Routine

In winter, the barns, and especially the outbarns, came into their own. Here was stored hay from the nearest meadows and here, too, were tied up young stock, which had to be watered and "fothered" twice a day. In the days before drinking bowls were fitted, watering the cattle meant turning them out, so that they could find water at a spring or beck.

The hard-won hay was eaten; and as the winter weeks went by

a large heap of "muck" was formed. This must be led out when the ground became firm again in late winter or early spring.

As the year waned, and Christmas approached, a pig which had been fattened to 20 score (and was therefore far too fatty for today's taste) was killed by a visiting butcher and the products—fresh meat, black puddings and sausages—featured at some memorable meals.

Tom Cowking says: "We would contrive to get off school on pig-killing day to watch the operation. Hams, shoulders and sides were salted, but all the offals had to be prepared for immediate use, there being no fridges then."

It was a calamity if the pig had received a shock just before being killed and the meat was inedible; or if the salt did not "take" and the bacon remained uncured.

First-footing

The Daleheaders were superstitious at the New Year. They liked a lucky, and preferably a dark-haired man, to "let t'New Year in." Usually, that person was Tim o' t'Park, or Timothy Robinson of Stephen Park.

Frank Dugdale related that some housewives forbade their grown-up sons and daughters from going out on New Year's Eve unless they undertook to be in before midnight. If they were still out at that time, they were locked out until the arrival of Tim.

Off To Church

The seats in Dalehead Church have been well examined and nobody need stay away for fear of them breaking.
T W Castle, Vicar (1916).

I was at the last service held in the parish church and recall the congregation standing about in groups afterwards. Dalehead folk, who had gone away reluctantly when the reservoir came, were back for an hour or two in what was left of old familiar haunts, and they were having a job to drag themselves away.
Frank Dugdale (1958).

ST JAMES's Church, Dalehead, built in the Early English style beloved of Victorian architects, was originally in the parish of Slaidburn.

Its great days were before the 1914-1918 war, when faith was rock hard and church attendances high; when the vicar's word was law and children were "Shining for Jesus":

Are you shining for Jesus, dear ones?
You have given your hearts to Him;
But is the light strong within them,
Or is it but pale and dim?
Can everybody see it—
That Jesus is all to you?
That your love to him is burning
With radiance warm and true?

The Slaidburn and Dalehead Monthly Magazine [a new venture for the two parishes] contained nuggets of information about everyday life. In winter, many a meeting was badly attended because of "inclement weather".

74

In 1911, when the Vicar and Headmaster at Dalehead were the Rev John Heslop and T A Deadman respectively, the Dalehead Glee Union was expected to take part in the Temperance Concert at Slaidburn but did not come "owing to the weather". The weather had been grim in the previous December when a concert party arrived from Nelson.

Three marriages took place during 1910. Henry Carr, of White Hill House, married Eliza Clark, of Tosside; William Rawsthorne took to himself Mary Hannah Robinson, both giving Cocklet House as their address; and Wilford Parker Robinson of Whalley was "wed" to Hannah Slinger of Greenfold.

Accounts for the Sports Tea Party showed a balance in hand of £4.1s.7d. Among the expenses were "Mrs Deadman, for dish broken, 2s.6d" and "Mr Woolf, for attending boiler, 4s."

In the summer of 1911, Dalehead celebrated the Coronation with a procession which followed "the usual route on such occasions, headed by the Slaidburn band." Halts were made at The Vicarage, Chapel House, The Grange, Bridge House and Stocks. At each halt, the children sang the National Anthem and "God bless the Prince of Wales". Coronation mugs were distributed. A free tea, sports and fireworks followed.

In 1912, the Rev F R Hawker Soper was inducted as Vicar. He came to Dalehead with a good record of work in London and Liverpool.

His parochial letters followed the style already set, being full of platitudes with nothing of real interest. The hay crop of 1914 "has passed averagely good, I have been told, and the weather for getting it in not so bad; at least it might have been a great deal worse"!

Slaidburn and Dalehead established a War Fund, with sewing meetings. Mr Deadman's children contributed "toffee money" to the fund and Miss Jennie Cowking of Lamb Hill raised £2 for

Princess Mary's Fund. Among the gifts donated were 50 shirts, 62 pairs of socks, 36 belts, 29 mufflers, 56 pairs of mittens, 11 pairs of cuffs and a chest expander.

So to 1916 and the ministry of the Rev T W Castle. The energetic Mr Deadman was succeeded as Headmaster by W T Price, who "comes to us with an excellent character and splendid testimonials." He followed local tradition by agreeing to be the honorary choirmaster.

When Mr Castle left a mining parish to come to Dalehead, he was presented with a gig and pony, which the parishioners felt he would need in such a wild place.

The Vicar told Frank Dugdale: "I knew little about farming, but soon after I got to Dalehead a farmer taking a beast to market stopped and asked me what I thought he'd get for it. I prodded it in what I thought appropriate places and guessed £18. It made £17.15s or some such figure. Ever after, I was regarded as an expert."

Announcing a Good Friday show of "lantern slide pictures", he observed: "The Church will be dark and there will be no need to 'dress up'." The parish magazine reveals that Dalehead Women's Guild knitted socks, mittens and mufflers for the Forces.

The Vicar, anxious to improve Church attendance, invited them to consider Churchgoing from two points of view—outside and also inside. He knew that Sunday in a farming community was not altogether a rest day for everybody.

"There are horses to be fed, cows to be milked and little pigs have a way of squeaking for their food. Still, the same animals eat on auction mart days. By a little arrangement most people can get to Church once a Sunday if they so desire..."

Stormy weather affected attendances at the Harvest Festival. "The morning congregation was fair, but nothing short of a fish would have ventured out to the Evening Service."

War service made its demands on the youth of Dalehead. John Swale, organ blower for many years, joined the Army. So did William Rawsthorne, who lived at Hollins, and William Carr of White Hill. News came of the death of Private Percy Hodgson. The Vicar reported that Joshua and Tom Hodgson had left home to join the Army.

Mrs Robinson of Swinshaw and Mr Dawson of Halsteads had kindly carted fuel from Clapham Station to the Church free of charge. Two or three more loads of coal and coke were needed. "Who will help us to get in our full winter's supply?"

During 1916, the telephone debt (£1.12s.5d) was cleared by the Fylde Water Board. It was a good year for the Church financies, money being raised to clear off the Lantern debt [for the projector used for Lantern Services]. The Knitters of Dalehead continued their war effort by sending off 73 pairs of socks and 26 pairs of mittens.

A Sale of Work was held on "a dreary, dismal day, rain and wind, then wind and rain...the sort when even millionaires feel poor" but inside the building was "a nice feeling of comradeship, brisk trade, piping hot tea, home-made cakes and country butter, with everybody cheerful and obliging."

The two Carr boys who joined the Army made the "the great sacrifice". A memorial service was held. "There had never been a congregation like it in our little Church," wrote Mr Castle.

Tom Cowking remembers that when Mr Rose, the curate of Slaidburn, took occasional services at Dalehead, he walked the round trip of six miles. At that time, the Vicar of Slaidburn was the Rev T C Garnett, a popular figure in the farming community. His love of farming led him to attend the sheep shearings at Catlow and Lamb Hill.

The long winter was broken by social events, including a lantern lecture given by an emissary of the British and Foreign Bible

Society. The projector operated by acetylene gas was provided by Leonard King-Wilkinson of Slaidburn. The smell of gas added to the excitement generated by seeing images on the silver screen.

Clergymen did not stay long at Dalehead (see the list of names with dates among the appendices of this book). The Rev Hawker Soper, a bachelor, lost the loyalty of the Daleheaders and before long was seeking a new parish.

Excitement swept the valley with the arrival of a Church Army caravan, a splendid vehicle which was heated by a solid fuel stove and had Biblical quotations painted in large letters on its sides. Three horses were needed to haul the carvan and the parish being visited had the responsibility to provide a site for a week's stay, a room in which meetings could be held—and board and lodging for the two Army men.

So cordial was the reception and so effective the witness that one week extended to six weeks. And when the Dalehead people waved the two young Army men off, they were not to know that one of them—the aforementioned T W Castle—would return to them as their Vicar.

The Vicarage, a fine example of Victorian architecture—and far too large for a parish like Dalehead—stood in capacious grounds. Mrs George Robinson told me that her father, who hailed from Bridge House, used to transport coal from Chatburn railway station to the Vicarage and the Schoolhouse. "It was a day's job to go to Chatburn down those winding lanes by way of Holden and Copy Nook."

Doris Wells, who left school at the age of 13, went cleaning at the Vicarage for two or three different vicars. "There were stone floors on the ground floor, and there were no carpet sweepers. Mostly the bedrooms had some mats on the floor. You took them down the stairs, carried them out and gave them a good shaking. You used a handbrush round the sides of a room and then got the long brush."

The Vicarage had attics and cellars "but I never went down in the cellar."

The incumbency of Mr Fryer is remembered. "We used to have to go from school and weed his garden. It was mostly grass with herbacious borders. When it was going to be the garden party, we had to weed. One day we were gardening when Mr Fryer arrived. He had a beard and a member of the weeding party said she would love to stroke his beard. He promptly gave her permission to do so.

Mrs Fryer, a kind sort of person, supplied the children with cups of tea and gave them buns. As Doris's brother once said, "By gum, she can burn buns. They're nearly always black." The Vicar's wife had worked abroad amongst other nationalities and "you had to do as you were told."

The regular attenders at Church included a contingent from Stephen Park. Vic Robinson had an unusual view of Church services, occupying the organ-blower's seat for two years. His sister Drina was the organist. Mother "never missed on a Sunday morning, wet or fine."

Vic remembers both the Church and its attractive setting, with an avenue of trees, including a weeping ash, with trailing branches. The tree may have been sawn off at some time to create a special effect.

In 1925, they took the Vicarage down, stone by stone, and used it to make the Boardroom at the southern end of the reservoir. "They tell me they built it as near like the Vicarage as they could."

When, with the reservoir construction work well in hand, it was decided that the church would be demolished and the bodies in the churchyard re-interred, the old inhabitants of the district felt a double loss.

Tom Cowking recalls: "Not only were they evicted from their

homes, but their loved ones were also moved from their graves. This caused much heartache."

Stone for the boundary wall of the new graveyard came from a local farm. The topstones and gateposts were brought from Jumbles Quarry, near the source of the Hodder.

The new graveyard was consecrated by the Bishop of Bradford in November, 1926, and the transference of bodies took place in the following year. The remains of the Daleheaders were reverently placed in large pine coffins and moved to their new quarters at dead of night, using a horse and flat cart.

One who saw the process said: "They had a storm lantern on the cart so they could see where they were going. It did look weird."

The School-house.

Unwillingly To School

A NATIONAL Endowed School, built at Dalehead in 1872, succeeded a charity school which had been owned and financed by the squire of Slaidburn. The schoolmaster at mid-century, Edward Hine, taught the Three R's and English grammar. His wife, Elizabeth, instructed the girls in knitting and sewing.

The new school, assisted by grants from church and government (£13), could accommodate sixty children but usually had about forty. The peak number, 72, was recorded during the time the reservoir was being constructed.

A distinguished "old boy" was James Hanson, the founder of a "milk empire" in Liverpool. At the age of nine, he went to live at Catlow, his grandfather's farm, and became a scholar at Dalehead. He walked two miles to school. Of special memory was a snowstorm of 1885, which left six feet high drifts.

He left Dalehead school at 13 with no special accomplishments except, it seems, the ability to addle [earn] money. He was generous towards good causes in the Hodder valley, donating silver trophies for competition at the show. He retained a love of Dalehead and was fond of recalling his days here.

In the early days of Dalehead School, parents had to pay for the education of their offspring. The Schoolmaster's house was impressively large for such a remote area and was therefore coveted by anyone applying for the master's job, which carried a salary of £100 a year.

Dalehead schoolmasters were usually "gentlemen and fine scholars", to quote John Walmsley. John also told the story of an unhappy choice. During one vacancy, three men were summoned by the school managers for an interview. A horse and cab were hired to collect them from the train at Clapham and convey them over Bowland Knotts.

Only two candidates presented themselves and one was tentatively selected. As the managers rose to leave, the third candidate arrived in a second cab. The managers went back and the interview proceeded. The man's credentials were outstanding and he answered their questions well. He was appointed Headmaster of Dalehead.

"Someone must have given him good testimonials to get rid of him," John Walmsley reflected. This man, who had said he was leaving a better job for the sake of the health of his wife and six children, was fond of strong drink. Whenever possible, he walked six miles over the Knotts to drink at Clapham—until his credit ran out.

Lurid tales about the Schoolmaster circulated through the parish. A burglary at the Schoolhouse was reported when the master's wife was away from home. Mr Walmsley and a neighbour investigated, finding the place had been ransacked.

Upstairs, sleeping a drunken sleep on a heap of blankets was the Headmaster. When he was awakened, and his attention drawn to the untidy state of the house, all he could say was that he had been looking for his false teeth.

Shortly afterwards, he announced that he had got another job. Nobody asked how or where. There was no one to cheer him on his way.

At Dalehead school, absenteeism was seasonally high. Even quite small children were expected to give a hand on the farm and it was not unusual for children to be kept at home when seasonal tasks like haymaking demanded the maximum labour force. If a girl was absent on Monday, it was presumed she was helping mother do the weekly wash.

Children living at the remotest farms walked over three miles to school and in wet weather their sodden top clothes were draped around a stove to dry. The stove was also useful when warming up food for the lunchtime break. The big kettle had a song in its heart.

When lessons were over, the children trudged home—Carrs from Halsteads and Whitehill House, Harrisons from Bottoms and Hindley Head, Robinsons from Catlow and Stephen Park, Cowkings from Lamb Hill and Rawsthornes from Hollins.

Ivy Waddington (nee Carr) grimaces at the recollection of walking about two and a-half miles to school. Mother prepared food in a large basket "which had a lid" and the children "used to get to falling out as to who should carry it. Sometimes we dumped it and collected it on the way home. Eh, but we did have some do's with that basket."

The school building had no architectural pretensions. It was box-like, with a steeply pitched roof. Inside was one large and one very small classroom. The Schoolmaster lived in the adjoining house.

Dalehead education was without frills. The teachers concentrated on teaching the Three R's (reading, riting and rithmetic!). When the school was first opened, the usual leaving age for a child was thirteenth.

Tom Cowking went unwillingly to school. He who had been reared at a quiet old farm where there were no handy playmates now found himself amid the noise and bustle of the classrooms.

"The big boys were swabbing pieces of blotting paper into the inkwells and using the wooden rulers as projectiles to flick the inky blobs across the room towards the desk of the woman teacher, creating a blue halo effect on the back wall. When a direct hit was recorded, the teacher grabbed a handy bar of wood and threw it at the class."

The teacher, who was of retiring age, had poor eyesight. When she left, a temporary master was appointed. This burly young man rang the bell at 9 a.m. Few acknowledged its summons, so he lined up the laggard pupils and caned them.

When Tom Deadman was appointed headmaster, the school inspectors' reports were excellent. He was a good headmaster, with a pleasant wife and a daughter named Evelyn.

Towards the end of Eva Walmsley's schooling, the Headmaster was Thomas William Price. His wife, who assisted him, arranged for people to give her old stockings, which were "cobbled up" and set aside for rainy days when farm children arrived with wet feet. "They had to change into the dry stockings until their own had dried," says Eva. "Mrs Price also used to dry your clothes for you. She was good that way."

The boys were rough at playing rounders and football. A Daleheader recalls: "Everyone wore clogs and boys, who had bumps and bruises, were quite often limping." Occasionally, the older boys had a "sheep gathering". They crowded the young lads into the lavatories and let them out one by one to be taken to a shed.

Here two boys, sitting astride a form, laid the lad between them, on his back. He was "clipped" and "dipped" and suffered other indignities before being released.

There was also an encounter with gipsies, probably German, who were hawking pottery round the villages and farms. "These gipsies had baskets on their arms and large basins or chamber pots on their heads.

"The sight of a chamber pot bobbing above the schoolyard wall was too much to resist, and one lad was dared to throw a stone. At the first clang, the gipsies put down their pots and gave chase, but we were prepared.

"We rushed into the porch, put a nail in to hold down the latch and hid under the coats hanging on the pegs. When the gipsies looked through the window, everything appeared normal but we certainly felt jittery if ever we met any hawker-type fellows when we were alone."

School inspectors who planned to visit Dalehead School entrained to Long Preston or Chatburn and completed the journey by hired trap. A school manager who was fond of visiting also had a pony and trap, which he persuaded a schoolboy to hold for him while he was in the school premises.

On one of his visits, thinking to stump the country children, he asked: "What's twice naught." A boy who put up his hand and was then invited to talk said: "Please sir, that's what you give us for holding your horse."

On the annual sports day, the Daleheaders congregated at the school, where a procession formed, headed by the Slaidburn Silver Band, conducted by Mr T Cowking. Now began a tour of the handiest farms.

Tom Cowking recalls: "First we went to Hansons at Bridge House, then back to Swales at the *Travellers' Rest.* From here we crossed the stepping stones to Cowkings at Grange Hall, Lords at Chapel House and Robinsons at Swinshaw.

"At each call, the band played a selection of tunes. The children received fruit and chocolate. The bandsmen disappeared into Grange Hall for a short time—I suspect for stronger refreshment—and on our return to school, dinner was served.

"We then went to an adjoining field, which was appropriately named Gambols Fold, for the sports. One sports day the vicar refused permission for the school to be used for serving tea and a barn was used instead, the sports being held in a nearby field."

Mr E Buck, the Clitheroe photographer, recorded the crowning of the May Queen in the school yard in 1913. He regularly cycled from Clitheroe to Dalehead in the years before the Flood. A heavy tripod was strapped to the frame of his bike and the cameras and heavy glass photographic plates were slotted into a special bag.

For the May Queen ceremony, the group consisted of two donkeys with traps, which were decorated with flowers and ribbons, providing an unusual but attractive setting for a queen and her retinue.

A man who began his schooldays shortly after the 1914-18 war was taught by "Daddy" Price. Nicknames, which were bestowed on everyone, included Clicket, Dabby and Spud.

A lad who sneaked up to the teacher's desk and poured the contents of two inkwells—one for black ink, one for red—down a hole in the desk, defacing the contents, was asking for trouble. He was not disappointed. "I never saw anyone get a lacing as he did."

Mr Killick is recalled as a Headmaster who had "a lovely head of hair, one mass of curls." He, too, was short-tempered. He gave a few "lacings" but "I don't think they did us any permanent harm...and we left school knowing how to read and write."

For the Coronation of George V, celebrations at Dalehead consisted of sports followed by fireworks. During the display, a thunderstorm developed.

Dalehead children also attended the larger, more exciting sports held at Slaidburn on Whit Monday—an event which attracted people from far afield. The Band led a procession to the home of the squire, Mr King-Wilkinson, where each child received a new sixpence.

George Robinson attended school in the days of William Price. "When father went, it was Mr Deadman." He was a stern disciplinarian, quick to use the cane. "They could do with chaps like that today."

Nine o'clock (prompt) was the starting time. "If we were five minutes late, we got the stick. If we got some spelling wrong, we'd have to stop behind and write the correct spelling 250 times."

George also remembers when the oldest lad in a family—if he was old enough—had to see to the clogs. He checked each one "to see that all t'clog-irons were fast."

Scholars attending the school in 1920, when Miss Fryer was the teacher, had surnames which had long been associated with Dalehead—Taylor (Sydney, George, Frank), Walmsley (Eva, Tommy), Hanson (Robin, Dennis, Harry), Carr (Doris, Bessie, Harry), Swale (Nellie, Tommy), Cowking (Alwyn, Titus), Robinson (Victor, Francis), Harrison (Lizzie, Frank), also Marton, Blackwell, Tivey and McPrice.

A member of the Wilshaw family, attending school in the 1930s, when Mr Killick presided, remembers when he "roamed about the village at mid-day, marvelling that before long the area would be under water." He also marvelled at Mr Killick's 7 hp Jowett car, though it did have trouble getting up some of the local hills.

Mr Killick was himself an impressive sight when roused, for he was Welsh, with a quick temper and verbal fluency. One of his former scholars recalls him, with respect, as "a ginger-haired, fiery Welshman." His wife, in contrast, had a retiring manner and was somewhat "mousy" in appearance. The Killicks had two sons, named Glyn and Merlin, and when (after they had left the valley) a third son was born, they brought him back to Dalehead for the christening.

When the schoolchildren of Dalehead were taken for a day trip to Blackpool, all piled into two cars. "I remember that day well. It was the first time I'd had potato crisps out of a packet. I was sick. We'd never seen owt like Blackpool."

Some of the children from Dalehead walked to Slaidburn on Whit Monday, which was Sports Day. Doris Wells and her brother went on foot from Halsteads to Slaidburn and joined in the busy social round. They attended a service in church and then walked to Whiteholme, the home of the Wilkinsons, for a silver sixpence. Returning to the school, they each had a bun and drink of milk.

Doris remembers the sports events, held in a field near the Church, with the strains of the Slaidburn Silver Band to put a spring into the heels of the competitors. Being just thirteen years old, Doris was able to compete in the classes for "over twelves" and "under fourteens". She returned to Halsteads on foot with "into the teens of shillings."

When Doris left school, she had an ambition to learn confectionery, having often helped her mother to make bread and bake pasties. Some girls were taught at shops in Settle. Doris asked her mother if she could go and learn. Said mother: "Ay, I don't think so. Ask your Dad." So I asked my Dad. He said: "Nay, lass, thou'll have to get some wark."

Years later, with both her parents dead, Doris—looking through some family papers—realised why she could not be sent to learn confectionery, remembering that in those days she would have had to lodge and actually pay for the training. "My Dad couldn't afford to send me."

Many remember Lily Pickles, the last permanent infants' teacher at Stocks. She was born at Shipley in 1890, passed a scholarship for Salt Girls' High School and also the Oxford examination for teaching (in 1905). She was married in 1914 and, after the war, came to Stocks, first lodging at Stephen Park.

In November, 1931, the Stocks School being threatened with demolition as the reservoir work came to an end, Lily Pickles was offered a job at Slaidburn School.

Mr Killick became headmaster at Shelley, near Huddersfield.

The slow lapping water of the reservoir crept to within a hundred yards of the playground as the reservoir filled up. Dalehead school was pulled down in 1933.

Chapel House, Dalehead.

Dam Builders

*In a few months, this quiet valley became a hub of activity. The
sound of locos shunting, the drumming of the power house engine
and all the other sounds, seemed to transform us into another
world.*
                                                        Tom Cowking.

I liked t'owd spot. It should never have been flooded.
                                                Farmer at Stephen Park.

SURVEYORS and engineers of the Fylde Water Board visited
Dalehead in 1910 to assess its suitability for a reservoir. The
Board supplied Blackpool and Fleetwood, which were among the
boom towns of the Lancashire coast.

   The Daleheaders stared at the motor cars which ventured into
their little valley and came to a halt outside the *Travellers' Rest,*
where for the next two months the surveyors were provided with
hospitality by John Swale.

   Everyone saw the surveyors because they collected information
about all the becks and runnels. Initially, it was proposed to build
four reservoirs, which were named Hesbert, Greet, Croasdale and
Stocks. The engineers arranged for trench marks to be dug, in-
dicating the high water levels of each reservoir.

   The summer of 1911 being dry and hot, the Board was forcibly
reminded of the need to enlarge the area of supply. Their response
led to the Fylde Water Board Act, 1912. No one thought to tell
the ordinary folk of the valley what was in prospect because virtually all the farmers were tenants.The Board's officials dealt directly
with the several landowners.

   John Walmsley was to recall a chance encounter with the chair-

man, solicitor and engineer of the Fylde Water Board. They were having a look round. "Mr Bickerstaffe, who I think was chairman, wore a cap like a ship's captain. Folk reckoned he must be on some business which was terribly official. One tale was that an Army camp was to be established at Dalehead. It was a long time before we knew they were going to flood us out."

The Water Board had "done its homework", commissioning reports from such notable geologists as Professor W Boyd Dawkins and Professor R H Tiddeman. Henry Rolfe was the consulting engineer.

Tom Cowking recalls a visit from water engineers to his father's farm in 1912. "They requested permission to sink boreholes in one of our fields. They said they already had the landlord's permission, so father could not object."

The equipment consisted of two heavy machines, one a steam boiler with an engine on top and the other a boring machine. Each stood on iron wheels and was horse-drawn from a newly-completed reservoir on Bleasdale Fell, the journey taking a long time because the machines had to be moved up the hills and lowered down the inclines with block and tackle.

When they reached the nearest point by road, these machines were moved down the fields on sleepers. It was tediously slow, being spread over several weeks. The operators found local lodgings and farmers were employed with horse-drawn carts to transport piping and coal to the site.

Finally, steam was raised and the job got under way. Men with spades dug shafts about eight feet by nine feet square, the shafts—maybe half a dozen in number—going down to bedrock and the soil, in wooden buckets, being wound up by windlass. Samples of the rock strata were packed in long wooden boxes.

Nature had been good to the Fylde Water Board by smearing the sides of the valley with impervious clay. The local gritstone was suitable for making into facing blocks.

The 1912 Act empowered the Board compulsorily to purchase the land in the proposed water catchment area, and this took place by private treaty. John Heap, a cashier with Fylde Water Board, recalled that the wealthier landlords employed solicitors and thus haggled and hung back for a better offer. The farmers who owned their own small holdings, and who could not afford to have professional advice, had to accept the first offer.

The Board purchased 9,750 acres at a cost of £150,000—or £15 an acre—having calculated the value of each farm according to the rent paid for the previous 20 years.

In August, 1912, the folk of Slaidburn were startled by the appearance of charabancs and private cars, led by the Water Board's splendid Enfield Landaulette, conveying a 90-strong party of officials and councillors from the Fylde coast to view the site of the proposed dam. The party were on foot for the last stretch of their journey, this being a round trip of three miles.

When the sightseeing was over, in the early afternoon, the return procession of vehicles took place, the cavalcade stopping at Whitewell so that the party might have a substantial meal.

The 1914-18 war prevented an early start to the reservoir-building. Afterwards, when a more detailed geological survey was made, it was considered safe to raise the high water level at Stocks, thus increasing its capacity to the figure which had been set for all four. Only one reservoir was therefore required. Permission for this change was granted in the Fylde Water Board Act, 1925.

The men who had been engaged in driving boreholes filled in the shafts and built huts to house the machinery. Those men who remained at Dalehead—J. Leeming, H. Lawson and a civil engineer known to the local people as Mr Fernside—lodged at the *Travellers' Rest*. Mr Fernside pegged out the extent of the reservoir and then arranged for a shallow vee-trench to be dug around the affected area, a distance of about nine miles.

By the Springtime of 1916, over 30 farms had been acquired and the Board had its legal access to the route the main aqueduct would take. It was about this time that the Board, having purchased the *Travellers' Rest* from John Swale, used it to accommodate visiting officials and engineers. By 1919, the whole village had been bought up. The smithy was used as a workshop until another had been constructed near the dam.

Anyone re-visiting Stocks Fold in the early 1920s would have been startled by the changes. What had been a quiet village now reverberated with the clatter of a train, for a siding had been built to connect with the temporary workshops.

Where, up t'steps, the youth of the valley had met socially in a Reading Room there was now a billiards table. Anxious to retain its labour force, the Board even provided a tennis court and a pavilion.

How to get the varied, bulky supplies to Stocks called for imaginative planning, which involved rail and road transport. In 1923, a railhead was established at Long Preston, with a depot near Tosside, from which lines of three foot gauge extended to the points of major activity.

Fylde Water Board took over responsibility from the Settle Rural District Council for five miles of the road between Long Preston and Slaidburn and operated a Foden steam lorry as far as Tosside.

The road to Tosside took considerable punishment as a traction engine, towing a trailer laden with sleepers and baulking [big timbers], moved nearly axle deep in ruts. "They were making some mess," recalls a local man.

Such heavy traffic led, after six months, to a costly renovation. The road was pitched with limestone taken from an outcrop at a nearby farm. The farmer also derived an income from hiring out horses and carts to deliver the stone to the road. "Yon chap med a fortune," it is recalled. The Water Board used Greenfold, below Hesbert Hall, as the site of a sawmill and canteen.

An amusing interlude at this time was the acquisition of an ex-Army hut to be a community centre at Tosside. The hut was at Skipton. Robin Waddington recalls that his father was one of those who organised its transportation, in sections, using horses and carts made available by his farmers.

The young lads were told to stand by at Tosside at 10 p.m. to help unload the sections of hut. When midnight came and went with no sign of the convoy of horse-drawn carts, the lads dispersed.

Robin was roused from sleep in the middle of the night by the return of the horse and cart, with Dad, somewhat the worse for drink, lying in the cart and in full song. "Usually he never took much strong drink." The horse had made its own way home.

The inebriated farmers had simply dumped the sections of hut wherever they felt inclined. "The men had to turn up next day to side it."

For over a year, a single massive pile of wood was all that could be seen of the new Tosside hall. Navvies, making their way from Long Preston to Stocks, got into the way of stopping nearby for a brew. They made fires from handy pieces of wood, selecting the lining boards, which were tongued and grooved and of a handy thickness for burning.

The pieces of hut remained as one heap for over a year before being assembled.

The narrow gauge railways were crucial to deliver supplies at such a remote site as Stocks. The depot at Tosside ("just below t'chapil") was known as "Tram" or "Tossit Yard" and apart from the rails consisted of just a few huts. "At first, some navvies lived in 'em."

Vic Robinson, who lived at Stephen Park, recalls: "They started on the other side of the river when they came at first—up the Greenfold fields. Then they had to bring it up Black House side. They came right through our meadows, which were at the back of the house." Another local says: "They didn't care tuppence where they went. If they wanted to go—they'd go!"

At Stephen Park, the new line was a nuisance. Vic recalls: "A lot of our meadowland was on the low side. We had to make crossing-shops to get horse and cart and all the machinery we wanted in haytime."

Two of the newer steam locomotives had local names—*Stocks* and *Hollins.* A tip wagon held about two tons. Larger wagons were used mainly for the conveyance of coal from Long Preston station.

On Sunday night, a procession of navvies might be observed between Long Preston and the waterworks. The men cut across by Stephen Park, where there was "many a feighting do" between the farmer and the most brazen of the workers, who made tracks through meadows just before haytime.

"You get about twenty or thirty navvies going across your land

95

and then see what a heck of a mess they could make. They wouldn't stick by the footpath."

Vic Robinson remembers when Stephen, his father, went out to remonstrate with three Irishmen. Vic, then only a lad, went with him. An Irishman told Dad to go to hell. "Aye," said Dad, "thee do t'same—and I'll show you t'way in a bit." Which he did, flattening all three men.

One of the Irishmen said, as he departed: "I'll have it in for you." Dad said: "I'll be here." Subsequently, a tough-looking customer turned up at the front of the farm, where there was an acre devoted to the growing of corn. The stranger trampled the growing crop. Dad went to remonstrate with him. Without a word, the stranger knocked him to the ground.

The Irishman had been as good as his word, finding an ex-boxer to represent him at Stephen Park. Vic says: "I can see him now. He had an arm as thick as my leg. He could roll mi Dad over just like a shot rabbit." Dad called for the gun. "My sister set off with it and a couple of cartridges." The stranger picked up his jacket and departed...

The Dalehead residents soon began to recognise individual members of the engineering staff, which was presided over by Mr Harry Cottam (resident engineer). His wife, who had been a buyer in one of the big Manchester stores, adjusted her life style to that more suited to the "back o' beyond". They had two sons, Jack and Brian.

A tragic accident led to the death of Brian. Father, two boys and Mr Atkinson, a deputy engineer, had been fishing in the river. The railcar they used for transport was devised with the engine situated between two sets of seats.

When the railcar was stopped for the points to be changed by Mr Cottam, Brian—unbeknown to the others—disembarked. When the railcar was being driven off, he was run over and so gravely injured he died several days later.

His grave might have been the first to be dug in the new burial ground at Stocks, but this plot of ground had just been consecrated and looked like a field. So, at the request of Mrs Cottam, her son was buried at Slaidburn.

George Robinson, who went to school at Dalehead, remembers some tomfoolery concerning the railway. What began as a ruse almost got out of hand. One of the lads attending school said he knew all about the wagons. He proposed that he and other lads, including George, should get into a wagon and travel a short distance. He would then apply the brake—and they would clear off.

The brake of the wagon on which their eyes were fixed was defective. One of the wheels was spragged with a piece of metal about the size and appearance of a sword.

Four or five lads clambered aboard, the sprag was withdrawn and the wagon began to move with a quickening *clickety-clack, clickety-clack* until it was travelling so fast that no one dare look over the rim because of the rush of air.

"That wagon took us right away down over Honeymouth Bridge (which was then a viaduct and is now all under water) and then we came to an up gradient and the wagon began to slow down.

"And who should be coming the other way but Mr Cottam, the chief engineer, driving his petrol-driven railcar. He took us right away up, passing Greenfold, and left us in a siding. Then he sent word to school what he'd done. The teacher was waiting for us. Heck—we did get into bother."

One route connected the mains works with Jumbles Quarry, near the source of the Hodder. Jumbles yielded vast quantities of gritstone which was used to pitch the inner surface of the dam.

Rail track was not easy to come by in those troublesome days of industrial depression, when none was being manufactured. The engineers toured the country, buying up surplus lots. Pieces of track were used to reinforce the strongroom at the offices!

John Heap once said that £250,000 was spent on preliminary work before construction work at the dam could begin. The reservoir house and boardroom were built of stone from Grange Hall and other demolished properties.

Tom Cowking comments: "In the old days at Dalehead, when there was no moonlight, it seemed pitch black. But with the coming of the power house providing current for the outside powerful lights, the reflection seemed to carry for miles, with the effect of moonlight."

Grange Hall, built on a bed of gravel which was several feet thick and covered a large area, had a rail siding of its own. A steam excavator was put to work. Trucks collected the gravel for use on the works. During the process, Grange Hall "fell into the excavator bucket and was carried away."

Says Tom Cowking: "When I visited the site later, I saw just a muddy swamp where this fine old building had been. Gone were the lime trees, the largest in the district, which stood between Grange Hall and the stepping stones." When the lime blossom was out, the trees were "full of bees".

New Close, Tom's old home, built in 1872, had been demolished and the debris carted away in trucks on the Jumbles Quarry line. "I wonder if the planners ever thought of the feelings of old inhabitants on seeing this devastation. People are not like stone, to be knocked down and re-built."

For the construction of the actual dam, the first step was to excavate a "trench" in the proposed dam centre. This trench was a few yards wide but went the full length of the dam and down to bedrock, a depth of about 100 feet.

The excavated soil and rock were hauled up by four electric cranes, to be tipped into railway wagons and carted away. Heavy timber shuttering was used to shore-up the sides of the trench for safety. The trench was then filled with clay to ground level and afterwards to the very top of the dam as construction proceeded.

This clay was puddled (worked by hand with spades and water to ensure it was watertight). Suitable clay, found nearby, was so tough that compressed air spades were used.

The "puddling" was a most unpleasant job. The puddlers stood in water all the time. Water was continually being poured over the clay so that it was workable with spades.

As the core continued upwards, towards the top of the dam, backing on each side was provided by soil, stone and other material which had been excavated from a place within the limits of the proposed reservoir.

Jumbles Quarry was the ultimate experience during the construction of Stocks reservoir. The turnover of labourers was considerable. Quarrymen left their lodgings at Hollins at about 6.30 a.m. and travelled to Jumbles in open wagons.

The driver, usually Walter Blackwell (Wally), had been out of bed much earlier. He and his wife lived at Hasgill and he had a walk of three miles to Hollins, arriving in time to have his locomotive in steam by 6 a.m. At the end of the day, he had the long walk home, over ground so rough that he was not able to use wheeled transport.

The men both quarried and dressed the stone. "At that altitude, in wintertime, only the strongest men could stick the job." Jumbles was a veritable refrigerator when the north wind blew, but the stone was exceptional. "All t'Filter House was made from it. Board Room's all built from it. Both embankments were built from Jumbles stone."

George Robinson gave me the names of some of the engine-drivers on the Jumbles run—Jack Porter, Wally Blackwell, Bob Mount, Bert Filer, Bob and Bill Dobson.

Apart from the driver, a locomotive had a "rope runner", a term which may have originated in the shipworks. He was the man who literally did the running about, hooking on wagons, changing points and, when he was not otherwise engaged, greasing the moving parts of the locomotive.

Coal for the locomotives came, as did virtually everything else, "down the line from Long Preston...very little stuff came the other way [via Slaidburn]; it all came from the top side."

If any navvy up at that quarry got the sack, the engine drivers had instructions they had not to give him a lift. He'd to walk back. Long Bob (Tisley) sacked the entire quarry gang of 36 men—and replaced it, on the following day, from the vast "reservoir" of labourers desperate for work.

Almost every road in the district had its shuffling tramp-like figures inquiring from local people about the location of Stocks. At its peak, the labour force reached just over 500 men. Most of them were housed in Hollins village.

The tipping of material was chancy in bad weather. "The railroads on the dam top tended to sink and sometimes an engine would tipple over into the soft mud. It was a major operation, involving gangs of men with ropes, to get it back on to the rails."

The tramway lines at this point were temporary and could be slewed into various positions to provide new tipping areas. Tom Cowking recalls: "This operation was carried out by gangs of men with so-called slewing sticks, which were placed under the rails. On the shout of the ganger, a heave together moved the line over."

As work progressed, the line which ran along the valley floor was now taken up and a new one brought into use on the south-east side. The route lay to the west of Stephen Park, crossing the road just north of the present burial ground west of Black House Farm, and terminating at Hollins village at the east end of the dam.

As for the dam itself—the main object of the exercise—this was

built with clay as the waterproofing material. "They were lucky to find a lot of good blue clay; they had their own puddle-field," says George Robinson. "They tipped it into a big trench, water was teemed into it and it was puddled in."

George Robinson, aged fifteen, was one of seven or eight full-grown men who were working for the Water Board, using a horse and cart to move stone for the road over the viaduct, where Bottoms Beck joined the reservoir. He received 1s.6d a load, and the money was handed over to his father, who owned the horse and cart.

Says George: "Bother struck up! The other men said it wasn't fair that I should be getting the same wage as them. The foreman referred the matter to the big chief, an old navvy, who came on Friday with the wages. The ganger told him; 'We've trouble in t'camp. Some of 'em are grumbling about Robinson. He's only fifteen and he has same wage as them'."

The "big chief" asked, drily: "Is he 'odding t'bloody job up?" The foreman reported that he was as good a man as any of them. He said: "I'll go across to them chaps." They were sitting round. "Now you b------, he said, what's this bother about?" One of them said: "I don't think it's reight."

Said the "big chief": "If tha's not satisfied, t'lot o' you can go down t'bloody road. And that's that!"

It was the end of the carter's rebellion.

Stocks Fold.

A Shanty Village

The town that grew up at Hollins. . . may have been the last word in industrial relations in the 20s, but today's counterparts. . . would have mistaken it for a Siberian work camp.

The men of Stocks thought themselves lucky to have a cinema showing silent films, a canteen selling anything from a packet of pins to a side of beef, a recreation room with billards and limited cottage accommodation for wives and families.

Graham Johnson (1976).

Hollins village was a little hive of industry in those days.

Eva Robinson.

A TEMPORARY settlement of large wooden huts, roofed with corrugated iron, was hastily constructed near where the valley was being plugged by a dam of stone and earth.

Seventeen living huts were set down in orderly lines, each hut being named unofficially after the resident family who lived at one end and had a number of lodgers in the other part of the building. The name of this shanty was derived from that of a farm, Hollins House.

To John Heap, a Water Board official who lived in a farmhouse near the works village for most of the eight years, the hurly-burly atmosphere of Hollins had more in common with the pioneering days in the Wild West than that of an erstwhile quiet Bowland valley.

George Robinson recalls that some of the navvy lodgers of Hollins were good cooks. He had seen a man cook some beef or ham on his shovel, using an outdoor fire. The shovel, kept in an immaculate state, and shining like silver at the start of each day, made an excellent frying pan.

The navvy would swill off the dirt and throw a large piece of prime meat on to the shovel, holding it over a fire which was made on the ground and was used for warmth and making tea, using a "three legs" from which a cauldron was suspended. The attendant lad was known as the "drummer up".

An extension of the railroad ran up the main village street and was used for delivering coal, collecting dustbins and, most importantly, for transporting beer to the canteen cellar, the line running directly into the cellar and the barrels being rolled out of the wagons on to side benches and connected to pumps in the canteen above.

The canteen proprietor, James Wilkinson, held a monopoly on the sale of provisions—meat, groceries, etc—at Hollins village. This place was a-wash with strong drink, though the Water Board did their best to ration the men to two pints of beer each lunchtime.

Hard liquor was banned but, as John Heap told a visitor, they made up for it by drinking enough beer and stout to sink a battleship. Some navvies ate lots of kippers "to give themselves a thirst."

If a man got fighting drunk, he spent the night in the "cooler", a covered railway wagon which was normally used to transport groceries and other goods from Tosside to the canteen. If, next morning, a man was judged to be still "incapable", he was taken along to the police house at Slaidburn, thence to the courtroom at Bolton-by-Bowland.

The cost of strong drink accounted for a large proportion of a man's wage of £2.25 a week. Out of this sum, he had to pay for his food and lodgings.

The workforce was cosmopolitan in character. Tom Cowking chatted to a navvy, for whom drink was his master, and he said that his brother was a Bishop. Another worker, who was popular when parties were held, would fill his mouth with fluid, either petrol or paraffin, taken from a flask. He would wait for a few seconds for it to warm up and then exhale, holding a match in front of his mouth. The vapour ignited and the man resembled a human blow-lamp.

The farmer at Hammerton Hall had a contract to deliver milk to Hollins village and this was done in all weathers by Cyril and Colin Hully. The route to Hollins from this direction could not be negotiated by wheeled vehicle and so the milk was poured into special cans for transportation on horseback.

It is recalled that the horse and attendant had to travel up a rough incline and cross a river, which was the only practicable way. "It is a wonder that the milk was not butter by the time it arrived at Hollins," says Tom Cowking.

The housewife in charge of a hut provided meals, if requested. She also washed clothes and made up the beds. The charge for bed and breakfast was as low as eight old pence. The hut-keepers bought local produce—eggs, milk, butter, cheese—from the Dalehead farmers, who for a while had a period of prosperity.

Taylor and Hughes, the Clitheroe confectioners, delivered a vast quantity of bread to Tosside for the use of the workforce. Augmenting the diet in season were trout which had been "tickled" where they had lain in the Hodder and its tributary becks. Navvies poached on a grand scale, the bags including pheasants from the woods.

The Fylde Water Board was obliged to provide a small hospital—a splendid white-painted building, complete with verandah. There were rooms for the patients, the surgery (the middle section) and resident nurse, Mrs Kirkby, her husband Bert and their son, Alan.

Eva Robinson, who enjoyed visiting the cinema, was forbidden by her father to cross the area of the dam at night on her way back to Black House. So she stayed overnight with her friend Mrs Kirkby. Sometimes, an impromtu dance was held with any patients who were mobile, the music coming from a gramophone.

A canteen was constructed, and it was possible to convert the main hall into a cinema or a dance hall. For the "pictures", an entrance fee of fourpence was charged, a similar amount covering tea and biscuits at the interval, when the projectionist changed the reels.

Providing a musical accompaniment to the otherwise silent films were three or four musicians—piano, violin, flute, banjo or drum. On other occasions, Rose Green, whose father worked at Stocks, played the piano to accompany the films.

In the early "talkie" period, Robin Waddington and his mate, Harold Metcalfe, had an hour's walk to get to the cinema from their farmhouse homes near Whelpstone Crag. "The films, which were mainly about cowboys, were primitive things in those days. We thought they were great."

Some of those attending the cinema, returning to their homes at night, saw lights flickering in the vicinity of the old graveyard as bodies were being exumed behind tarpaulin screens and borne by horse and cart to new resting places near where the new church was being constructed.

An alternative to the Hollins cinema was that in Clitheroe. "We left our bikes in a shed near the centre. It was at our own risk. One Saturday night, my brother had his bike stolen. Whoever took it left in its place a rotten old painted up green thing. I can still see the look on my brother's face when he realised what had happened."

Tom Cowking recalls an exciting journey home after a visit to a dance at Hollins village with Alice, the young woman who became his wife. As noted, Mr Cottam had a railcar. There was also an attendant four-wheeled, flat-topped bogey, controlled by a brake stick, which might or might not be attached to the railcar.

Mr Cottam departed from the dance early, taking the railcar but leaving the bogey to be used by anyone who did not want to walk far when the dance ended at 2.30 a.m.

"After the dance, there were so many people waiting for a lift it was impossible for all to fit on the flat top. Then someone suggested that we might lie down flat, one on top of another, and in this way all could be transported!

"We launched off. I was at the bottom, face down over the front of the bogey, with a great weight of people above. We were all wedged so tightly that the man who was nearest the brake stick was unable to use it properly. Soon we were travelling like an express train.

"As the wheels clattered over the points, sparks flew up into my face. I hoped that there was no cow asleep on the track. All went well but it was a long time before we forgot an experience which was like being on the Big Dipper at Blackpool."

John Heap recalled to a newspaper correspondent that once a month every seat in the cinema was unscrewed and removed to make room for a dance, "which attracted not only officials, their wives and gangers, but local farm workers." The journalist, adding a bit of colour to the story, had the farm workers "still in their muddy work boots and reeking of manure!"

Local people were able to attend events held here. There was an annual Farmers' Ball, attended by up to 600 people. It began to raise money for Blackburn Infirmary and was so successful that Stephen Robinson, as the oldest tenant and one of the most active supporters of the dance, was made a life governor at Blackburn.

His son, Vic, recalls that the women of the valley produced a mountain of food. "Some ladies boiled ham or beef. Others baked. And yet others made lemon cheese. It was all dished out at supper time."

107

The band of five or six players was under the leadership of Alec Pinington, who had an administrative job under the Fylde Water Board. He played the piano. Walter McLester was on the drums. Another well-remembered player was Banjo Billy.

"We danced from eight o'clock till three o'clock in the morning. Then on Monday night we had an eating-up do. There was often so much stuff left over it had to be sold by auction."

Tom Cowking recalls that people attending on foot "could be picked out by the flicker of their lanterns and shippon lamps. They came across the fields from distant farms." Others were conveyed from the top of the dale by railcar and yet more came in a special coach pulled by a steam locomotive.

"To see the locomotive with its special coach standing at the door awaiting its passengers at 2 a.m., with black smoke coming from its chimney and steam blowing-off with a loud hiss, reminded me of films I had seen about the old Wild West."

Another regular dancer says: "You could hardly stand up in t'place, there were that many folks. They came from Clitheroe and all over. They used to run a train from Tosside across country. You caught train just below t'chapil at Tosside. It was nice and clean. Wagons were covered in and they'd put planks in for folk to sit on. That train got you through, but it was a bit bumpy, I know that..."

Incidentally, the last Farmers' Ball of the series took place in the Cinema at Hollins Village on February 10, 1933. As usual, the proceeds went to Blackburn Infirmary. The newspaper advertisement included the note: "This is positively the last Ball we shall hold, as the Cinema will be demolished after the event. It is our desire to make this effort a Grand Finale."

The music was provided by A Pinington's Full Orchestra. The tickets cost three shillings, for a gent, half a crown for a lady, and included a knife and fork supper. Secretary for the event was J Walmsley, of Black House Farm.

In 1923, more men were recruited, the majority being of Irish origin. It was a good time for an employer of labour, which was cheap and abundant. Few questions were asked. A bad worker might be sacked on the spot.

If rain set in during the forenoon, and looked like continuing, the works whistle would blow at 1 p.m. This indicated there would be no more work that day. The men were forced to sit mournfully in the hutment at Hollins, waiting for the sky to brighten.

A worker who had been in the Army during the 1914-18 war spoke bitterly to Tom Cowking about Lloyd George's promise of "a land fit for heroes to live in." The worker said it had turned out to be more like a slave camp.

John Heap recalled to an emissary of the *Lancashire Evening Post* that when the 720-yard long outlet tunnel was being constructed, the men sustained eight hour shifts round the clock, which meant "one following another into the same bed." When the tunnel was completed, the bosses threw a potato pie supper and donated a barrel of beer.

Beer was a consolation. Men quickly wearied of the routine in a back o' beyond setting. They drowned their sorrows in Dutton's beer, fourpence a pint, brought by rail via Tosside. If they were still sorrowful, they moved to another civil engineering project. It was the opinion of John Heap that if there had not been an adequate supply of beer, the dam would never have been built.

Harold D Bowtell, in his book *Lesser Railways of Bowland Forest and Craven Country* (1988) gives many details of Hollins, which succeeded Greenfoot as the residence of the workers. The first four residential huts, with gardens, were completed in August, 1923.

The hospital had three main sections—ward, treatment room and living quarters for Nurse Kirkby and her husband, who was the site storekeeper.

The cinema, which opened in December, 1924, showed silent films, projected by the ubiquitous John Heap, the piano accompaniment being provided by Alex Pinnington (who was in fact one of the joiners).

The canteen, a lengthy building, completed in the summer of 1923, had separate entrances for the general canteen, foremen, the "cafe" and general shop, which (with the licensed canteen) was managed by Jim Wilkinson. A smaller building held the butcher's shop and food store.

Mr Bowtell relates that meat for the butchery department of the shop at Hollins came from Newton. Bakers delivered bread daily to Tosside, from which place it travelled to Hollins, with other necessities, by the narrow gauge railway. Railway wagons loaded with barrels of beer arrived weekly by train.

Hollins had a football team which played in the Craven League and one year won the cup. The team was managed by James Wilkinson and then by Jack Green, who looked after the shop and canteen (and married Nancy Moon). Soccer enthusiasts recall "a little fellow called Tivvy" who was "all ower t'field and, by gum, he could score goals."

In summer, cricket matches took place. A bowling green was established.

Most of the workmen had left the village by 1932. The last of the huts, still named after the Collinson family, remained in situ until the 1940s, when it was being used as a workshop.

The opening ceremony, on July 5, 1932, was by Prince George (later Duke of Kent). He pressed a button to open the valve and admit water to the aqueduct. The reservoir overflowed on March 3, 1933.

John Heap vacated the farmhouse he had occupied. It was earmarked for demolition. He organised a sale of furniture and brought in prospective buyers from Slaidburn by bus. Luck was not on his side. The sale made less than £60, the bedding on display outside having been burnt by a chimney fire.

Bridge House.

Stocks Today

When I look out over the water at Stocks, I can't help wondering
how it was possible that a whole valley and its inhabitants could be
moved, lock, stock and barrel, without compensation, except for
the few who left at once. Even they got only a token payment.

Tom Cowking.

They got their notice to clear out. Some were lucky and some were
unlucky. Stephen Park and a few others were lucky. The water
didn't reach us.

Vic Robinson.

IT IS said that the first boat to cross the reservoir held Mr Cottam,
the resident engineer. He asked his chauffeur to drive the boat.
The man was willing but he knew little about it and, after a while,
inquired: "Where's the brake?"

Vic Robinson was among those who watched the dam fill up,
"but it took a while. We could see the water backing up to where
the island is now. It used to be just a hillock.

"They'd used tractor and chains to pull down buildings. A lot
of the stone went into the viaduct [which carries the new road east
of the reservior]. They pulled out trees, roots an' all, and dumped
them on our land. There was an acre of nothing but big roots.
They didn't care anything about damage. They were ruthless..."

At the time of writing, large areas of the catchment form a con-
ifer forest. The Forestry Commission, granted a lease of 3,000
acres of land in 1949, planted the first blocks of trees in the vicinity of Stephen Park, keeping to the old field patterns and leaving
the drystone walls.

Farming of a sort had continued after the opening of Stocks

112

reservoir. Vic Robinson, who was brought up at the 400-acre Stephen Park, recalls: "When the Fylde Water Board came, they split the farms up and they put two farms [the Greenfolds] to us; we would then have about 1,000 acres.

"We had about sixty head of Shorthorn cattle, and a few black ones, but the stock was mostly sheep. Being on a gathering ground for the reservoir, our cattle mustn't go near the water. The fences belonged to the Water Board, but if any stock was seen near the water, we got a letter from Blackpool—remove the cattle at once!"

The sheep were "a crossed lot." Dad crossed Swaledales with any sort of ram. "He wasn't really a sheep man; he was a horse man. I liked to get a good ram and then you hoped you were going to have some decent sheep."

After some years, the 11-month lease was not renewed—and in came the Forestry Commission with its massed conifers.

One notable building with pre-Flood associations is the new Church of St James, which stands just out of sight of the reservoir which displaced its predecessor.

The Fylde Water Board met the cost (£2,000) of dismantling and rebuilding the church. They also paid for the exhumation and re-interment of 150 bodies from the old churchyard. (Thirty of the bodies, being unidentified, were buried in a special grave).

Graham Johnson, writing in the *Lancashire Evening Post* (1976) after meeting John Heap, mentioned that one of his most vivid experiences had been "the gruesome ordeal of exhumation [which] still sends a shiver down his spine... In the sinister shadow of flare lamps, they removed tombstones and crumbling coffins behind hastily erected hessian screens..."

The work, which was much less dramatic than the newspaper article implied, was carried out with great decorum by Banjo Billy, who first arranged for a supply of strong pine boxes for the remains of the dead. He organised the work so that it took place at dead of night, between the hours of 1 a.m. and 4 a.m.

The new church, with its Early English style, featuring a capacious and steeply sloping roof, bears a superficial likeness to the old church. The big difference is the absence of the chancel at the east side of the nave. The present church has a stubby appearance.

When the reservoir was completed and a kindly Nature began to heal the scars, John Heap hoped that strict controls would be applied before steps were taken to provide access, adding: "It would be a big mistake to let tourists and trippers roam free."

John Howden, the grandson of Jack Green, who was works foreman at Stocks from 1919 until 1932, was born in the building which had been the hospital at Hollins village. His grandfather had been responsible for fitting the woodwork, including the oak panelling, in the Board House, which is on the terminus of the railway. It was built of stone from the old Stocks Vicarage and was formerly used to accommodate visiting members of the Water Board.

Mr Howden was at Stocks during the 1939-45 war. "Among the first things I can remember is that the Germans appeared to use Stocks, which is a large expanse of water, as a navigational aid. At least, they seemed to come over to Stocks and then turn southwards towards Manchester and Liverpool.

"My mother always used to say it was possible to identify German planes by the sound they made [the engines had a wavering note]. Quite a lot of planes flew over from the East Coast to the Barrow area.

"I remember standing at the window of my home and watching two of our planes flying over very low. At the time, the fells were misty. I saw a huge flash of light and apparently those planes had crashed into the top of Burn Fell. I remember my father rushing home—because he was in the Home Guard—to help with the rescue party."

The area had Army activity and tanks lumbered about the district. John Howden began his schooling at Slaidburn in 1944. He remembers that before he set off to walk from Stocks to attend his lessons his mother put cotton wool in his ears.

Scrapmen have lifted the rail tracks from the famous Jumbles Quarry but could not recover remains of the steam engine because a lively beck has cut a gully through the area.

The red Post Office van which daily flits from one farm to another is the successor of Shanks Pony. Mr Rawsthorne, the previous postman, had a three mile walk from Slaidburn to Dalehead and then a long delivery round before returning to Slaidburn. Frank Dugdale remarked that the postman ensured that nothing happened at Slaidburn that wasn't known the next day at Dalehead—and vice versa.

What is now the Ribblesdale Estate at Long Preston was the site of the railhead, from which incalculable quantities of material were conveyed via Tosside to where the dam was being made. A local lady told me that the Fylde Water Board purchased the land from a Mr Bentham. Local people still call that area, which was developed for housing, "Water Board".

When the reservoir work was completed, the Daleheaders had scattered. Most of them did not travel far. Doris Wells told me: "My Dad bought a farm at Rimington. We hadn't a clue where Rimington was, only that we had to turn off at Chatburn..."

Epilogue

It was a sad time for Dalehead. Families were forced to leave their homes and farms one by one. Some were lucky and managed to find places nearby. Many had to go miles away. Our village was split up all over the North.

It was a sad time for Dalehead. Families were forced to leave their homes and farms one by one. Some were lucky and managed to find places nearby. Many had to go miles away. Our village was split up all over the North.

Vic Robinson, formerly of Stephen Park.

BLACKPOOL, Fleetwood and the Fylde got their extra water supply, at a cost of three million pounds—and the loss of a community which had endured for over 1,000 years.

The Daleheaders were a spirited, self-reliant, somewhat isolated people who had come to terms with an area where the weather was often grim and every blade of grass must be coaxed from the cold, wet soil overlying the glacial clay.

The farmfolk and villagers were helpless against the might of Fylde Water Board, with its powers of compulsory purchase. It was acquisition by stealth.

The Board employed the best consulants and solicitors, whereas the farm folk, with no spare cash, could not hope to have professional advice.

Farms which were not in a flood-zone were none the less abandoned because they stood on the catchment area. They became memorials to a vanquished people.

Farming of a sort might have continued, as it did for a while in a modified form, but the Water Board followed the now discredited course of allowing the catchment area to be planted up with trees.

Most of the Dalehead community was now in exile. Tenant farmers who had no compensation settled where they could. Mrs

116

Cowking, of New Close, with her few cows and sheep, had to adjust her farming to Black Moss, where the land was quite different from that she had known.

Stephen Park was lucky—for a while. "We were just over the hill," says Vic Robinson, who with his wife Annie, a native of Tosside, have lived at Pepperhill Cottages, Bolton-by-Bowland, for well over 30 years.

He was still at school when the bodies in the nearby graveyard were exumed and re-interred at the new burial ground. "They unearthed a wooden arm. The story goes that it had belonged to a farmer from Black House who lost an arm to a frisky stallion and was provided with one made of wood."

Vic Robinson, like many another Daleheader, is full of tales. He remembers when his grandmother, Anna, had a large rhubarb patch and in the growing season she baked rhubarb pies incessantly. One of the workers, sick of rhubarb, bravely scythed the patch flat. Anne was not beaten. "She made them bundle up every stick of rhubarb. It was rhubarb pie every mealtime for days on end!"

There were some rum (mischievous) lads at Stocks. Some of them, noticing that a farmer had entered the inn and left his horse and cart outside, unhooked the horse, put the shafts between the bars on a gate and then yolked the horse up again, presenting quite a problem for the drink-befuddled farmer.

I found indomitable Daleheaders at Rimington, Waddington, Slaidburn and Rathmell. They showed me faded photographs of a life that was. They were more than happy to share with me both the memories and the pictures of t'owd days.

The Fylde Water Board gave way to North West Water, which has been privatised.

Appendices

BASIC FACTS ABOUT STOCKS RESERVOIR

Construction begun 1921
Officially opened 1932 (by Prince George)
Embankment height 110 ft above river bed
    length 1160 ft at top
    width at base 678 ft
    width at top 20 ft

BRIEF PARTICULARS OF WORKS

(as compiled by the Fylde Water Board)

Area of gathering ground 9,259 acres
Top water level 596.5 feet above Ordnance datum
Total capacity 3,059 million gallons
Area of reservoir at top water level 344 acres
Distance round reservoir 6.2 miles
Maximum depth of water 103 feet
Quantity of water available for supply 13,096,764 gallons per day
Quantity of compensation water 6,548,382 gallons per day

LANDLORDS OF FARMS BOUGHT BY FYLDE WATER BOARD

Towneley Estates. Lamb Hill and Kenibus; Collyholme; Hollins; Grange Hall; New Close.

Bentham Charity. Hasgill; New House.

Williams, Atkinson and Procter. Stephen Park.

Rickard Trustees. Dalehouse; Fair Hill; Heights; Higher Halsteads; Lower Halsteads; Birch Hill, Old Ing.

George Clarke. Bridge House; Swinshaw.

J Hanson. Croft House.

Peel Brothers. Higher Birch Hill.

H L Hare. Clough Hall; Tenters; Bottoms; Hesbert Hall; Long Dyke.

E O Bolton. Cocklick House.

J Swale. New Inn.

J Robinson. Stocks Farm and Property; Smithy.

A BRIEF CHRONOLOGY

1911—Survey work and borings by Fylde Water Board at Stocks, Hesbert, Greet and Croasdale.

1912 (Aug 7)—The first Fylde Water Board Act relating to Dalehead receives royal assent. (Subsequent Acts in 1919 and 1925).

1915-16—Purchase by the FWB of wheelwright's shop and machinery owned by John Swale. Subsequently, the Board took over *The Travellers' Rest* to accommodate engineers and officials.

1919—Completion of the purchase of the village. First sod cut for the FWB railway sidings beside the Midland line at Long Preston.

1923—Completion of first four residential huts at Hollins shanty village.

1924—Opening of the cinema at Hollins.

1926—River Hodder diverted through tunnel to enable work on the dam to go ahead.

1926 (Nov 12)—Bishop of Bradford consecrates the graveyard where the new Church has been built. First interment (Nov 30) is a fifteen year old girl from Hollins shanty village.

1927—Exumation of bodies from the old churchyard and their interment in the newly consecrated ground.

1932 (July 5)—Opening ceremony at Stocks by Prince George (Duke of Kent).

1933 (Mar 3)—Stocks reservoir overflows for the first time.

1934 (June)—Auction sale of plant and buildings.

CLERGYMEN ASSOCIATED WITH DALEHEAD CHURCH
(Notice the brevity of each incumbency)

A Lancaster Curate (1852-3)

John Brodwell (1853-8)

James Yornall (1858-63)

A Ellenbeck (1863-6)

W Calas (1866-9)

H O West (1869-72)

J Novis (1873-8)

P Brown (1879-82)

E Holiday (1882-5)

W Woodward (1886-97)

G A Johnson (1897-1904)

J Wharton (1905-10)

I Heslop (1910-12)

I R H Soper (1913-4)

T Castle (1915-9)

J Fryer (1920-3).